Souls Of Light

A Personal Guide To Spiritual Transformation

Souls Of Light

A Personal Guide To Spiritual Transformation

Dr. Ronald D. Bissell

Inner Voice Productions
Saco, Maine

2/96

Published by Inner Voice Productions
Suite 2165
2 Saco Island
Saco, Maine 04072

Cover design and editing
Triamond Concepts
West Hollywood, CA 90046

ISBN 0-9639446-0-6

First Edition - 1994

Bookstore

"ONE COMPOSED OF MANY."

Virgil (Publius Virgilius Maro)

Table of Contents

Acknowledgements

There are many people who have influenced my life and given me direction and courage when needed. Mentors, spiritual teachers as well as those who through their unselfish love have given me so much. I wish to thank Joyce, Brad and Dan who have allowed me the time and space to pursue this avenue of learning. I thank them for their encouragement and complete trust in this process. I also give a special thanks to Eban whose wisdom inspired this journey into the Light.

Introduction

*"The whole purpose of the world seems to be
to provide a physical basis for the growth of the spirit"*

Goethe

The first step in anyone's growth is to recognize who they are and what their purpose in life is. How they recognize and discover this key is as individual as their personality. Each person has multiple interests and multiple choices in life. How they use this choice mechanism and direct their interests determines the direction and speed of their development.

In my case, I worked, studied, and became involved with healing. Over the past twenty-five years I developed a practice limited to Oral and Maxillofacial Surgery in a small coastal town in Maine. The rewards of such a practice are many. I am respected for my credentials and knowledge and am placed in a position of trust. This trust, however, is due to the mask of my position and training. What people do not understand is that the respect for outer credentials does not reach or touch the true respect that is needed in life: the respect for who you really are. This respect is an internal respect that comes by being recognized for your life's purpose, not your life's outer mask. This respect is needed in life in order to grow and mature.

When I began my practice, I found that stress became my partner and that an incalculable strain appeared in my life due to the responsibility for people's lives inherent in my specialty. This strain continually bombarded my mind and caused a great deal of anxiety. I needed to find a place from which I could live my life in peace. I needed to find a way to express who I was, and what my innermost thoughts contained. I needed to find that place where my true self lives and then begin to bring that self into realization. I found that immersing myself in my work did not bring fulfillment. By denying my innermost desire to achieve peace and harmony, I was distancing myself from what I truly wanted. It was when I recognized this split in direction that I began to turn inward to find who I was and what I wanted in my life.

As I look back, I see a continuity to my life that I could not see when I walked each day. I see life as a journey that has neither beginning nor end. I see a path open before me that I cannot comprehend but know intuitively to be present. It was finding and touching this path that led me to my present place in life.

I was born into a family where both parents were Protestant ministers. They lived a life that was different from most. They spent hours, days, years helping others and in turn received a great joy from life. I did not realize that in watching them I would be attending daily workshops on service, compassion and love. I would learn firsthand how to help others, provide sustenance to the weak and provide an atmosphere of love to those I contacted. It was after this "schoolroom" that I began the quest to understand my own desires to heal. I spent years learning techniques that allowed the healing of physical ailments while ignoring the inner healing that I desperately needed in my life.

I walk a road that is remarkably different from my parents, yet is it? In their case, they spent their lives helping others. They called on people in their homes when difficulties arose. They made night calls when tragedy struck. They spent time one on one talking about wounds that needed healing and events that needed repair. They discussed life and death as a part of the normal pattern of life. They healed, consoled, and repaired wounds where necessary and were a profound influence on the lives of all they touched.

I, too, spend hours dealing with others' difficulties and yes, even make house calls when needed. I spend a large portion of my time one on one with patients, heal wounds, influence decisions people make, and at times discuss life and death. It amazes me to realize and to admit that I, too, minister to others' needs. Perhaps others see my ministry as largely physical, however, I am convinced it is not the physical that needs healing in this world today. What needs healing is the inner turmoil and the inner disruptions that most people fail to recognize, or conveniently put out of their minds as they travel their unconscious paths.

Fortunately, I recognized early in my career that it is the inner self, the inner soul that needs to be awakened in every person. It is this inner awareness that provides the energy and drive to become all we can be. We can retreat into this inner space and remove the pain and misery that the conscious self creates in our life. It is this inner world that needs to be awakened to provide each of us a moment of refuge, a moment of peace.

I began my study to open into this inner world. By learning to meditate and by constantly entering into the inner world through meditation, I created the awakening of my inner self. By awakening the inner self I discovered the path to connect with others, the path of a larger world, a path of immense importance open to anyone. When we enter this world, we discover the self we forgot, the self that expresses the eternal. We find the essence of our past, the path that our life must follow, and we uncover the future. It is from this place that we begin to live our life differently and from which we influence all others.

Learning how to enter this world encompasses the journey into self. We each have control over the timing of this entry. The reward to all who begin to seek this path is the discovery of life. How many people take the time necessary to understand the path they travel? How many people look into their souls to discover their true nature? Those who do, rapidly become aware of an inner landscape that provides freedom and joy. They are the few who travel throughout their lives changing all they contact.

How do we enter this world? How do we begin the alteration of our present life and find the peace we were created to uncover? For centuries mystics and religious students have understood the need of the soul to provide communication with the conscious and unconscious minds. Through meditation, prayer, and inner quiet we approach and understand the larger world, as well as the inner landscape, and alter our future forever. My intent in this book is to help you understand this inner world by allowing my inner world to be heard. It will attempt to provide you with answers to questions that most never seek. In this process your inner world will become exposed and you will begin to find your path in life.

Each of us is a teacher, and as such we provide a source of immense knowledge to our world. When we allow our lives to give that knowledge to others, we begin to change the face of the world. In my case, that life changing moment came during one of many meditation exercises. I unexpectedly began to realize the potential that existed within my mind to enter peaceful and quiet states. I discovered how to place myself into a deep meditative state in order to produce calm and relaxation. It became apparent to me that it was necessary to recharge my mind to focus and center upon the tasks within my life. I also realized that I underwent a mental overload due to the constant stimuli I received each day. This barrage of stimuli caused psychological imbalances in my life and required adjustment at regular intervals. I found meditation and relaxation to be the key to this inner adjustment.

As I studied and continued with my meditation, I became exposed to spiritual realms hidden from my conscious view. I read many authors and through these readings began to understand my self and how it affects my life. I found that paths began to open that created joy and calm in my life. I began to experience what others would call abnormal feelings and thoughts, but to me they seemed normal and life-enhancing. Messages began to pass through my conscious mind indelibly leaving their influence upon it. The more I worked to understand these messages the more I was able to comprehend their effects on my life. Each message built upon the previous message and soon they began to show signs of continuity. They helped me travel through very difficult psychological and spiritual transitions. Each message gave very thoughtful and timely advice. The substance of these messages is what I wish to bring to the consciousness of this world, for in them I found the needed seeds to create a new world.

I am an ordinary person who experienced an extraordinary awakening. I heard messages that made me listen, told me incredible stories and forever changed the direction of my life. I realize now that the real world is outside my physical senses and that the veil of my seemingly all-knowing consciousness hides it from view. It is my hope that by reading and studying the ideas I present, readers will awaken that part of their mind that is asleep and begin to travel on a path that leads to the understanding of the real world. I believe that if enough people start to communicate with this world, the future of humankind will advance toward the Light—and change for eternity.

Light Seeds

1. What is your purpose in this lifetime and how has your life's course influenced this purpose?
2. List 5 reasons for your present position in life and 5 reasons why you are searching to change it.
3. List 5 things that your life has taught you as you have developed and grown.
4. In what way can you allow the universe to influence your life?
5. What can you do to bring the Spirit into your conscious mind?

1

Inner Journey

*"The value of life lies not in the length of days,
but in the use we make of them:
a man may live long,
yet get little from life.
Whether you find satisfaction in life depends not on your tale of
years, but on your will. "*

Michel Eyquem de Montaigne

I have always been a person who enjoys watching others. By watching other people's methods of treating each other and by listening to the way they spoke to their loved ones, I was able to develop an inner sense of how I could lead my life. As I watched, I uncovered many truths about life and saw many obstacles that had to be overcome in order to provide a life of peace and joy. I intuitively understood where to find strength and how to invoke that strength for use during needed moments. I saw that many searched in outward directions to satisfy the world's interpretation of success. I saw how they unconsciously struggled and perfected their ability to achieve monetary gain and to use others as stepping stones for advancement while living in a sea of unbelievable deception. All the while their lives consisted of broken relationships, hollow agreements, and forgotten ethics.

I struggled to make sense of this seemingly contradictory lifestyle. I felt inferior and thought that my world was a world gone wrong. I constantly put myself down while creating the appearance of calm. Inwardly, however, I struggled to keep my inner world together. It was during these moments of greatest distress that I began to understand the way to live my life. I began to listen to the quiet space within my soul.

How many times have you taken the time to listen quietly to the world around you? How many times have moments swept by when you could hear the song of the universe played out in your life? Have you listened? Have you heard the news given to you each day by the universe or have you ignored the messages? I found that it is important to listen for these quiet words, understand their worth, and foster their meaning in my life. By doing this, I began to perfect my soul and to understand my reason for being.

Why are you here? What role are you to accept and what are you to accomplish in your life? When we take the time to listen to our soul, we find the task before us becomes simple. We access that inner quiet and find it contains all the wisdom needed for growth. Obtaining this connection to wisdom allows us to hear answers to our life's concerns. It is by listening to these answers that we can follow our inner guidance and find the Creator's peace within us.

The Creator made us part of a divine species; a species that can learn both to be at peace and to grow into the unlimited space of love that surrounds us. Our task is to enter that space, hear its voice so we may follow its inner guidance, and show its love to all we meet. The guidance of this inner voice will provide the direction to our lives. Sometimes life's events hide that direction. How many times have you feared a choice when that choice has opened for you without conscious thought? Have you ever looked back over your life to see its logical progression? Realize the importance that this direction brings to your life and use it to create a world of peace.

What direction am I to follow? Where shall I go? How can I achieve the desires of my heart when the destination appears so distant? The answers to these questions were communicated to me through love. I experience this love as a glow of Light that transcends all barriers of time and age and creates a peace that encloses all that I need to grow and mature. I see this Light and use its power to transcend all the problems I face. I use it to help others and to inform their world of the way to live and conduct their life's journey. Spend time finding this glow of Light and begin to follow it, for in this Light you will discover your future. When you find and follow the Light, you will succeed beyond your greatest dreams and desires. You will realize that the Light guides you in all the moments of your life and will not allow you to fail. You can then travel along your path and learn to work with peace in your heart. You will remember that the Spirit is within you, is a part of your life, and that through peace and love you will succeed in your journey.

To succeed in life you need to relax and enjoy your present journey. By doing this, you will stay on your way in life, and you will prevent moments of failure from causing you harm. Envision that the today you see is unique and will never return, and that you need to enjoy each moment it brings. Then, understand that the future you envision may not occur; and that by enjoying each day you will allow each tomorrow to provide for itself. In doing this you will begin to realize the wonder of the universe. You will experience a sense of joy and provide a new opening into the future you desire.

The discovery of the truth led me to see my world expanding. I saw that the world of those who caused confusion in my life was not the only possible world. On the outside I saw the limitation of their ways and within myself I saw the expansion of my world. I saw the universe and in its expanse I witnessed the scope of the Creator's love. When I discovered the Creator's way in my life, I found a universe full of wonder and became filled with the feelings of peace and contentment. Once I discovered my path, I was attracted to its Light and continued to follow this Light on my quest.

I learned to honor Spirit with respect and reverence and began to live my life according to my newly-found way. I forgave others and did not allow them to influence my path any longer. I learned to leave them in their world in peace.

I found Spirit in all things, great and small. I felt Spirit within my being and realized it was the Spirit's presence that caused me to flourish. I found that materialism was not my way and that spirituality was the key to the inner peace and contentment I desired. I grew spiritually, and through this growth, freed myself from all the bondage I found on this plane.

In life,
all love,
all caring,
all things through the Spirit
are possible.

Wash away the fear,
wash away the hatred,
wash away the loneliness,
for you are loved.

Live each day in peace.
Find happiness
and walk within the Light.

Light Seeds

1. List 5 qualities that you have seen in others' lives that you wish to create in your life.
2. List 5 qualities you have seen in others' lives that you do not wish to see in yours.
3. What method or methods can you use to listen for words of wisdom?
4. How do you experience the answers to life's concerns?
5. List 5 lessons that you have discovered in your life.

2

Inner Needs

"My body is like a drifting cloud
I ask for nothing,
I want nothing. "

Kamo No Chomei

My path through life has been different from most. I have not sought fame nor riches, but have only searched my world for messages and clues to the eternal. As I search, I find moments of struggle; but, I also find moments of love. Each day, I work to see the Light in all things, take a path forgotten by many, and find that when I promote the way of the Spirit in my life, I cannot fail. I work diligently to overcome my weaknesses and take time to understand the things that produce a way of living that fulfills my purpose in life. I concentrate on my life and on my life's direction because I know that without this I cannot focus on my path. I speak of peace and harmony, maintain bonds of friendship with my soul, expect success within my heart, and work to encourage others along my life's path.

Welcome each new day with joy
and listen quietly for words from the Light.
Take time to wonder at their meaning,
for if you do,
you will accomplish great things.

Contrary to popular view, accomplishment is not the issue; life is. We chose our path to learn as much as possible during this time of passage. By learning, we undergo a transition that allows us to enter into our heart and become a great soul. We listen to love's whisper and to the feelings that are within our being, for it is there that we hear our inner voice speak. In doing this, we become full, we break the bonds that have kept our minds captive in the past, and we learn that by living in the present we will continue on our path.

When I understood these truths, I realized that within each of us there are needs that cannot be fulfilled by the external world. There are needs that must be uncovered to create a world of love. I saw these needs in me as the tools to permit the maximum expansion of my world. Take a moment and see if these tools are present in your world.

The Present Moment

The present moment is a difficult concept for many to understand. How many times were you present when someone needed your help? How many times have you failed to see the beauty that each moment brings? How many of us live our lives for future events that never occur and realize in the end that we missed out on life? How many of us miss living each day?

I find that living my life in the present moment is very important. When I fail to live in the moment, I lose my life's direction. Dwelling upon my past and reliving its moments causes me to lose the direction life requires. Likewise, focusing on the future dissolves the current direction of my soul. It is necessary for me to be present at all times so that I can listen to my feelings. I do this so that my feelings do not fade, but provide the direction I need in every moment of my life.

All exists in the present moment. The present is the reference point of life and encompasses both the past and the future. Welcome this moment for it allows freedom, peace and thanksgiving. It is within this moment that we become free. By working in the present moment, we focus on our present life, see the lessons we need to learn on our journey, and grow without limitation to fulfill our destiny. By focusing in the present moment, we will not become lost in the eternity of the past and future, and will not lose the direction of our lives.

Why not live in the present? Why not accept the Light it offers? Why not encourage others to do likewise? The answers to these questions are simple and are in the present moment. When I undertook the quest for the present moment in my life, I did not stagnate in the past or future, but uncovered eternity. If you live in the moment, you will discover that it is beautiful, comforting, wonderfully peaceful, exciting, and has boundless energy and feeling. It welcomes each event with enthusiasm. It is important to use the present moment to become all we can be because this moment will never return. It is also important to set within ourselves the vision needed to feel accomplishment and fulfillment in life.

Never forget your accomplishments.
Never forget to thank the Spirit
for what you have achieved in life—
for the support of the Spirit underlies all.
It is the Spirit that will see you through difficult times.

If you live in this moment,
you will endure.

Forgiveness

The thought of forgiveness brings up many different pictures in my mind. When I reflect on these images I question their validity in my world. Who should I forgive? Why? By thinking about forgiveness, I realize the need to turn my focus inward where true forgiveness can change my world. How can I live a life of peace when I blame myself for misfortunes in life? How can I remove the pain they cause in my life? When I turned within, I discovered the answer.

If you settle for forgiveness,
you cannot grow.

If you develop forgiveness,
you will.

Forgiveness must be sincere,
without regret,
and it must be from your heart.
Walking through life without forgiveness
will cause you to become saddened,
you cannot have peace,
and cannot feel contentment.
Therefore,
be sure to learn forgiveness so you can grow,
for through forgiveness all things begin.
Forgive your self,
forgive others.
Enter into the essence of forgiveness,
for the Light from your Creator
will shine its brilliance upon you.

When you live with forgiveness
your life will enter new states of being.

You will find that forgiveness is an ingredient essential to your growth. It is necessary for the continuation of life, for you must forgive to excel within. If you carry the burden of not forgiving your self, you will not rise above the problems of each day. Only by embodying forgiveness in your life can you see a different world. Therefore, walk in the path of forgiveness and instantly change your world.

It is the Spirit that brought forgiveness into the world. Learn from its example. Learn to be an example to others. Learn forgiveness. Don't wait until the events of life make you think of forgiveness. Simply begin each day with forgiveness. If you do this, you will find that these events will change in proportion to your ability to forgive.

> If you sow forgiveness,
> you will reap the universe.

Listening

I was with a friend the other day talking about life's ups and downs. We spoke of the need for quiet and the need for listening to our center, our heart, to live a balanced life. We took time to listen and compared the quiet to the chatter of words. We listened to the daily news report. Then, quietly listened to our hearts. Do you think we noticed a difference? We noticed that our hearts were warm and honest. By contrast, the news we heard produced sadness in us.

Begin to uncover your heart, listen to the words it speaks, and silently hear its murmurs. Do you see how it takes a special tuning-in to hear the small voices within your heart? By worshipping the Spirit within you can develop the amplitude to hear your heart.

> Take the time to hear,
> make the time to hear,
> and cherish the times you do hear.

> Listen to the earth,
> it will tell you much.
> Listen to the energy flow from the universe.
> Listen to the Spirit within for the silent news
> that will help you become a good listener.

It is up to each of us to fulfill our destinies by quietly listening to our hearts. Listening to this quiet will uncover the seeds that are necessary to lead us onward toward our goals and visions. These seeds are designed to be listened to and to grow from, and are to be used as guideposts toward the results we envision in our lives. Continue toward your goals and needs and work consistently toward their attainment. Listen and be prepared to undertake the needs that you discovered to grow. When you listen, you follow your inner voice and seek the presence of the Spirit in your life.

Welcome the listening abilities you possess
because you will always know when the Spirit is within.
You will feel its presence in your life
and will honor the knowledge it gives to you.
In this manner,
you will understand the needs of your soul.

When I embark with joy on the tasks I encounter in life, I learn to uncover the good in all things. I relish the thought of continuing on in my journey and feel and hear the messages given to me from the universe. Hearing these messages allows me to collect their knowledge and to nourish future learning events. In this manner, I grow from each endeavor I undertake.

I find it necessary to schedule a time of quiet in each day, when I can think the thoughts that only the Spirit can supply. Through these thoughts, I learn and grow tremendously, because by seeking and listening to the voice of the Spirit within, I can touch eternity.

Light Seeds

1. What needs do you see in your life that cannot be filled by the external world. List 6.
2. What value does living in the present moment bring to your life?
3. Why is forgiveness so important to your growth?
4. How can you arrange to listen to your inner voice? When? Where? How?

3

Inner Qualities

"A bell is no bell 'til you ring it.
A song is no song 'til you sing it.
And love in your heart wasn't put there to stay,
Love isn't love 'til you give it away."

Oscar Hammerstein

Many times I am saddened by the circumstances of my life. I become afraid, and this fear is a crippling blow to my life. I realize, however, that fear and sadness do not lead to life but lead to frustration and anxiety. Such feelings are a waste of time and cloud my life's direction. When I travel my path in happiness, each day becomes a new beginning. To do this, I start my day with love in my heart and the Spirit within my being.

I cherish the knowledge I uncover when I open my soul to my conscious mind. I find that doing this is the first step in removing the bonds that kept me hostage in the past. Using this knowledge wisely, removes any sorrow from my mind and helps me think thoughts of my tomorrows. These thoughts fill me with wonder and fulfillment about the future. When I follow the voice within my soul, I grow from within; for it is the voice of the Spirit. By constantly listening to this voice and following its teachings, I grow and receive the direction of my path. Remembering this simple fact allows me to grow tremendously.

Begin to search your self and see the good that is within it. Feel a new energy flow that will enlighten you and help you realize that inner peace is yours for the asking. Once you find peace you will move in the direction of your dreams and will work to encourage others and to enlist their help in your quest. By noticing the impact you have on them, you will know the direction you are heading in life and will see any changes needed in it. It is especially important to receive the help of those who share your qualities and your direction in life. This will help you strengthen your path and to realize that your qualities and direction create the world you see.

Happiness

Happiness, like joy, is all around us; but we must train ourselves to look for it. As we grow and develop we lose our childlike fantasy, and happiness can fade from view. Fortunately, it is lost only to our conscious mind. By taking time to reflect and calm our minds, we can return to that time when happiness was a part of our world. We can follow the Light from the Spirit to become happy, for the Spirit exists within each of us in varying degrees, according to the lives we choose. So, become confident that by following its teachings happiness will become your world.

I find that changes taking place around me are the direct result of my inner journey. These changes occur as I take time to meditate quietly and search my heart. As I meditate, I realize where my strength comes from and I feel the power which is liberated within me.

Imagine the stillness of a moonlit night.
Imagine a quiet presence in space.
Imagine the wonder of a clear summer sky.
If you are still,
you will approach the truth of peace.

Follow the direction of peace in your life.
Do not retreat,
but follow its lead.

Then,
work with peace in your heart
and study with the peace you will find
through the amplification of your joy.

In doing this,
your world will change,
your being will shine,
your essence will be felt by all you contact in life.

Patience

How many times in your life have you become upset or irritated at the apparent slowness of your inner desires to come to fulfillment? How many times were you startled into paying attention to the need to be patient? Do you walk slowly along your path and listen carefully to your soul? In our society we live a fast paced-life and do not take the time necessary to listen to the voice within our souls. It is important to learn to follow this voice and to hear its murmurs. Then, it is important to internalize what we hear in order to grow.

Encourage your mind to learn patience, for in this process you will discover that patience is an art you need to nourish. You cannot find patience in the world around you; you must seek it. By doing this, you will find that teaching patience is not possible, but learning patience is. Take the time necessary to develop the skills to learn patience and see how it gives you the quiet time needed to obtain plenty in your life.

Our society is logic oriented and logic-oriented people cannot quickly learn lessons in patience. In this world, we live for deadlines, schedules, workloads; daily, monthly and yearly quotas. How can we expect to master spiritual lessons when we spend so much time living in ways that prevent us from learning? That is why we need patience now. People need to feel patience, caring, and love in their lives.

Trust

Trust is necessary within the self, but it is very hard to develop. By looking carefully, we can see the seeds of trust that are dormant within us. Learn to cultivate these seeds so that they will grow into fully mature gardens. Can you trust your self? Can you trust others? Can you live without guilt or jealousy? Do you have patience? Think about these questions for you will achieve these qualities and more when you remove the limitations you place on your self. These limitations are the invention of the human mind and can become its downfall if you dwell upon them. By understanding these feelings of limitation, you will begin to sense the real need to expand and grow. Therefore, release the brakes you place on your soul, and know that releasing takes time and thought. It is this time and thought that most people will not accept as a part of their life's experience.

Remove time,
and you will have eternity.

Accept eternity,
and you will have the way to accept
all the thoughts of this universe.

The universe is endless.
The space within is timeless.
Forget time,
and the space opens up.
Open the space and look.
There you will meet your Creator.

Light Seeds

1. What knowledge have you uncovered by listening to your inner soul?
2. What changes have occurred in your life as a direct result of your inner journey?
3. List 3 examples when patience could have changed the result of events in your life.
4. Can you develop trust within your world? If you cannot, why

not? If you can, how can trust change the direction of your life?

4

Inner Focus

"Who is it that says most?
Which can say more
Than this rich praise
that you alone are you?"

William Shakespeare

I am amazed each time I look at my life's direction. This direction occurs without conscious thought on my part and has a pattern that can only be seen by a careful analysis of the events that occur in my life. I see that as I follow the direction presented to me during moments of quiet, I discover the inner needs of my life. I work to allow these needs to surface in my consciousness and to become a working part of my path. As I grow, qualities that I need to recognize gradually become noticeable and enhance the direction of my life. It is only then that I begin to realize the need to turn my focus inward to discover the real emotions of life. These emotions permit me to continue to grow and deepen my spiritual journey. I hear voices that constantly encourage me to grow, to seek and to continue on my path in life. They catch my attention and move me toward an inner world of peace and love. By listening, I discover my true self and find it to be an extremely important gift to my life.

Become who you are.
Become mindful
and listen to all the voices that are within you,
for you will learn greatly from them.

Become all that you are
and in doing this
enlist others in your quest.

We have great things to accomplish in our lives through the Spirit. By following its direction, we can overcome difficulties we find and learn to follow the principles it gives to us. We learn to listen to its voice and to watch closely the future that is presented to us. We especially need to listen to those who are sent to teach us the way and to walk with confidence using the knowledge they give to us throughout our lives. Then, we can work with all the information given to us to change and enhance our lives. This will allow us to begin our journey home.

There are a great number of lessons that we will learn in life. Many center on growth, while others deal with the need to incorporate the basic ingredients of life in order to provide the basis for growth and development. The three main ingredients are the development of peace, the discovery of self, and the feelings of love.

Peace

Peace is essential to all forms of life. To be at peace, it is necessary to be at rest and quiet within. Can you see how the Spirit's presence can be quieting to your mind and soul? Can you hear its voice tell you of your needs? See how you can obtain peace by listening to this inner voice. It is the voice needed in our world, and the place to seek it is within. Seeking the external in our world causes disharmony, whereas, setting our eyes upon the peace of our souls allow us to accomplish all things in our lives.

Through peace I learned to forgive others their faults and their lack of understanding. I also forgave my self for my perceived shortfalls and needs. It is essential that we become at peace with our selves, for in this peace all advancement is found. Therefore, it is important to surrender to the Creator within all the things that cause harm or discouragement. By doing this, we provide a place for peace to grow.

When we study our being, we discard the old ways we

have known and uncover a new way of living. With this discovery, we obtain harmony and walk within our souls to discover secrets known throughout the ages. And when we pursue the path to these secrets, we will find peace.

Old thought patterns act as stumbling blocks to obtaining peace in life. But they can be eliminated easily. All that is required is to interrupt them and to begin dwelling within your being. By doing this, you will start to become fully who you are. This is a powerful secret. We are part of an unparalleled secret of the universe—for within us is a reflection of the Spirit. We can notice this reflection when we take the time to see the peace it offers. When we fully choose to accept the peace it provides within, it causes us to grow. We each have the choice, and the choice is easy to make when we listen quietly for the Spirit's direction. Begin to connect your self to the choice to accept this peace, for once you do, you will never walk alone.

The knowledge needed to understand this universe is within each of us. Our Creator's wish is that we grow and become unlimited; to become unlimited in size and effect in the movement of eternity. Therefore, become quiet and listen to the Spirit, for the Spirit dwells within. There you will find the answers to life's dilemmas. Humankind's quest for outer gratification has led it to the despair we see around us. When life revolves around the materialism of this world, it cannot be at peace, but when life revolves around the Spirit, it will quickly move forward along its path. Therefore, follow the guidance given by the Spirit and seek its presence in your life. Tomorrow can be a new beginning. It can mark the turnaround you seek; for when you follow the Spirit's guidance, you will see great changes occur in your life.

Your way is secure.
Your way is correct,
just,
honest,
and good.

You can cross the boundary into the Spirit
and be welcomed into its realm.

You can seek and find.
You can encourage others on their path
and be at peace.
Because of this,
your life can change.

Begin to discover your needs
and learn your strengths.
Begin to follow your path
and rest within the peace of the Spirit.
This is the peace that passes all understanding.

Peace comes to those who are willing to seek its way. Peace is obvious to those who honestly seek its presence and acknowledge the Spirit in their daily walk. Thank others as well as your self for this miracle, and for your ability to become all you can be. You see, becoming all you can be is a difficult process.

When I followed the direction that the Spirit started in my life, I was able to rejoice in the goodness of its way. I prevented others from causing dismay or concern in my life, developed an intense inner peace, and became my true self.

Self

Start to understand the need in life for your true self to emerge. Many may say that they cannot understand their true self, however, I find that self is always present and is the paramount issue to deal with in life. If the true self is forgotten, life cannot continue. However, when you introduce your true self into all matters, you cannot fail.

Understand that self is to the person as air is to breath
and needs constant support and nourishment.
Discover that self can fail
if there is loss of hope and belief.
Therefore,
welcome the growth of self
because if you forget it,
your life will fade away.

Remember,
self is the all-important ingredient.
Self is to growth,
as salt is to pepper.
Self grows by allowing itself to be discovered.
When you discover your self,
you have grown.

Your true self is wonderful.
It is kind,
gentle,
compassionate and pure.
It is wise,
all knowing,
and special.
Your true self is known
and is created in the image of the Spirit.
It is like fine parchment
that has been carefully made and prepared
so that you can have your life imprinted on its pages.
Therefore,
hunger for the vision you seek.
Thirst for the knowledge it takes to undergo inner growth
and the search for wisdom.
For when you smell the fragrance of love,
you will discover that within is the love of creation,
within is the tapestry of life,
within is the peace of the worlds.

Live with this peace.
Do not let it go away.

Travel the path set before you
and understand that peace is necessary
on this earth to fulfill your place.
When you learn to encompass all things
with love and caring,
to encompass all things with support and feeling,
you will dissolve doubt
and become free.
You will understand that all things develop for good.
All things invite peace.

Therefore,
walk in the Light
and find peace and self.

Open your self
and you will open the wonders of the universe.
Do not forget self,
because self is the issue to understand.

Self is the issue.

Why is self so important an issue in life? Where is self
located? How is it found and liberated? Within each of us
is a self of unimaginable beauty, a self that has been present
for ages, a self that will endure forever, a self that is a direct
reflection of the Spirit. When you undergo transformation,
you open the self and unleash a new beginning and a new
perspective in life. Spend a few minutes in exploration of
self. In just those few minutes you will uncover the true
universe in all its majesty.

Working with the self allows us to overcome the evil
and misunderstanding we find in life. It creates motivation,
which helps overcome obstacles we think are impossible to

surmount. It is necessary to open the envelope of self and let the Spirit's Light fill it completely. Then, we can set before it the desires that are of importance to us so that we can read them into our souls, and in turn, receive the translation of the universe.

You can develop a self that can understand your inner journey and become a witness to the events of your day. By doing this, you will see your self in all you touch, will formulate your own reality, and will live within its grasp. You will begin to change your reality and thus change your world. You see, in life many realities exist at once. It is up to each of us to pick the reality we wish in life and live it to its fullest. When we focus on the realities that reflect the picture of our self, we will change the fabric of the universe. We will settle on the reality that encourages self to grow and will achieve the reality of our dreams.

Take a moment and step within your self and witness miracle. Step within this crucible of life and witness a change. Once you find and listen to the self, you can never remain unchanged. Your course will alter, your steps will become sure, your balance will improve and people around you will notice a profound transformation.

Within this space you will find peace and contentment.
Within this space is found the Spirit's presence.
Within this space is found the universe.

Start to remove the doubt,
remove the fear,
remove the anger,
remove any false self that may be within.
What is left is the true you without tarnish,
and it is good.

I watched the changes that occurred in my life once I began to align with my inner world. Opening my self allowed me to speak with my soul and to grow in unexpected amounts. When you find and open your soul within, your outer world will undergo dramatic change. These changes will signify the presence of the Spirit and will permit you to become the full self you were created to be. When you follow the feelings that come from the soul, your desires match your true purpose in life. Obtaining this wisdom allows you to use the knowledge of the past so you can securely pass into your future. Then, you will stop the doubts you have and will begin to listen to your soul.

It is when we proclaim the beauty that Spirit provides to us in our lives that we will open the doors to eternity. We will not ignore that part of ourselves that regulates our inner world or fall into the trap of ego and false self. We will endure, endure, and endure. We will continue on along our path and will not struggle with the questions of life. We will realize that what we are is true and whole, and we will thereby pass through life with the knowledge we obtain from our soul.

Love

Of all the topics we will discuss, I think love is the most important. It is the quality that rules the universe and is the lining of the vessel of life. It is the only force that can move the world into a new dimension and is the force that gives answers to all of our concerns.

Remember each day to love the fact that you are alive.
Love each moment given to you
and cherish every thought you create.
Live to love all living creatures.
Love the fact that you are aware of their presence
for most cannot express
or experience the miracle of love.

By allowing love to become a part of your life,
you will grow in the presence of your Creator's love.

In life, we need to speak softly of love but proclaim its goodness far and wide. In doing this, we will uncover love's vibrations whenever and wherever we are. We will cherish all thoughts of love, for we are not here to suffer, but are present to enjoy our lives. We are here to serve each other so that we may become all we are capable of being.

Remember that love is the breath of life.
It is the only thing all people understand.
Humankind accepts and responds to love
for it needs this emotion to survive.

Be love.
See love.
Seek the power of love.
Encourage the thought of love
and the need of love for others
for you can save the world with love.
Then,
enter into a covenant with your self
where you will only think thoughts of love.

Love others as you love your self.
Love your enemies.

Remember,
love conquers all.

Haven't you heard about love before? Why can't we listen to the whisper of love and listen for its presence in our lives? When we follow our hearts, what happens? We find love!

Love is in a burning ember.
Love is in a butterfly's wings.
Love is in the stroke of dawn.
Love *is*!

When we surround ourselves with love, we will not fail in life, but will undergo many unbelievable changes and will obtain peace from all of them. Therefore, tell everyone you meet about love's presence in your life. Do this by showing love to them through your actions and deeds. You will discover that love will thrive when you cast away your doubts about its presence. You will hear it when you speak of love in your life.

Can you see love in a rainbow?
Can you see love in each other's eyes?
Can you see love in a drop of rain?

All you need to do is look
and you will find love.

Love can settle all the differences we find in life, because love is the most powerful tool in life. It can be sent to all we see. We can find it in all things and realize that it forms the fabric of time. You see, without love we cannot exist. Have faith in love, for when you learn to stand firm and enter into life with love your reward will be extraordinary.

I forgive those who do not love me and pursue those who are in need of my love. I search for the parts of my life and work that are devoid of love, worship them and send them love, thereby, I remove the doubt of love's presence in all humankind. By listening to my heart, I find love's presence in abundance in my life. I see it as the creation that produces all. It is what all people recognize and what makes their life become new. By serving love to all I meet I am allowed to become free. Therefore, pour love into your self so you will become a crucible for service. Why is it so hard to understand? Why are there wars and fighting? Why can't we all be free? *We can't be free because love is not present.*

Follow love
and who needs war.

Follow love
and who can argue.

Follow love
and your world is renewed.

Follow love
and you cannot fail.

Begin to work for love
and seek its presence in your life.

Enter into the future with love
and you will see your true self appear.

If you partake of the banquet of love
you will never again be enslaved.
You will settle all your differences with its presence.
Work to search your heart with love.
Sing with love,
love with love.

Under all your thoughts become love.
In all your actions talk of love.
If you do,
you will grow tremendously.

Be thankful for love
and you will prosper.

Spend with love
and you will invest in your future.

Go with love
and you will not be forgotten.
For when you seek with love,
you will find your Creator.

State of Being

Take a moment to consider the thoughts that pass through your mind. Of what are these thoughts composed? It's important to consider this question, for in your thoughts is the knowledge needed to continue forward in life. Welcome them and work to use the knowledge they provide for the development of your world. The Spirit gave you this knowledge, and it is through its recognition that you will uncover the freeing of your mind.

As we travel farther along our paths, we hear things that will aid us in our spiritual growth. We walk quietly and quickly within our souls and take the time to look at our outer world to acknowledge the lessons given to us daily. We watch other people as they walk through their lives, we see how they relate, and through them, we learn to seek the vibrations of the Spirit in our lives. Doing this allows our eyes to open to see that growth is necessary in each stage of our lives and that such growth is essential to the fulfillment of our destiny.

I discovered that growth without wisdom was not a worthy goal to pursue. By working toward my goals and desires I developed the wisdom necessary to obtain the growth I wished. By working, I began to know my self better each day and began to learn that I must develop strength to overcome the burdens of everyday life. I learned that such burdens are present to help me grow and mature, for without burdens and problems, I could not see the way to live my life in peace.

Begin to dwell upon the present moments of your life and eliminate any noise or interference you may hear. By doing this you begin to achieve true peace, because it is the quiet that frees your mind to experience its presence. You will find that peace is not possible without the Spirit's presence in your life, for it is when you walk quietly within and find it's love, that you will achieve your true state of being.

I found that this state of being is in the direction of the Spirit, is determined by spiritual laws, and exists within my soul. When I approach this state, I find peace in an unlimited supply. Each of you can experience this peace. Do not be afraid of it. Do not feel that it is impossible to achieve, for when you forget the pain of the past and remember only the joy that peace can bring, you will find that there is no limit to the peace you can experience.

This state of being is similar to the feelings people have when they are deep under water. Can you imagine the buoyancy and the feeling of weightlessness? Can you sense that in this place your body does not exist as form? This feeling is your true state of being. You need to understand its form, understand the weightlessness of pleasure, and the lack of body, for your spirit is without body and without senses. It is pure energy and is without physical need. Start to take the time to feel the calm this state presents to your soul and examine the quiet it contains. Once you do, you will begin to understand that this calm can be with you always. All you need to experience it is to have the will to provide it space within your soul. Therefore, allow this peace to fully enter your life.

Move this day with a renewed confidence within.
Establish peace and security within your world
and work to achieve your goals.
By doing this,
you will enjoy the peace that this moment brings.
Do not allow the thoughts of this day
to become marred by the thoughts of yesterday;
only permit your true self to show.
This will be sufficient for this day.

Light Seeds

1. What is your life's direction? What encourages you to follow this direction? Where is it leading you?
2. List 5 changes that experiencing peace can bring to your life.
3. Why is self such an important concept to uncover? Describe your true self.
4. How can love change your life? List 5 areas in which love could transform your world.
5. How would you describe your present state of being?

5

Inner Changes

"Today is not yesterday.
We ourselves change.
How then,
can our works and thoughts,
if they are always to be the fittest,
continue always the same.
Change, indeed, is painful, yet ever heedful;
and if memory have its force and worth,
so also is hope."

Carlyle

We are created as social beings who look to each other for support and love. This support creates a network of interrelationships that makes it appear like our outer world is the important arena of life. We forget and become mesmerized by the glitter that the outer world provides. Once silence is achieved and we touch our inner soul, the need for inner change appears. This change causes a metamorphosis of great dimensions and alters the path we travel.

As a species, we are created with an immense joy within our souls, but over time we have learned to cover up its beauty. When we uncover this hidden joy, we resume the natural state in which we were created. When we focus and center on the Spirit within, we are able to reach this state and move our world into higher planes of existence. By doing this, we satisfy our desires for a better world and make our lives incomparable to those whose lives are scattered and fragmented. By changing our selves, we effect change in the world around us. I find that as I live in the direction of my soul, I lose the feelings of fear. I notice a calm that resides within me when I follow my inner voice. Have you ever noticed the calm that you can possess when you come from a centered and focused position?

At times we may become tired of the struggles in this life. However, do not allow your self to become dismayed when these struggles appear, because the progress we make in our journey becomes noticeable when we remove the fog that surrounds us. When we look at our lives from a distance, we will see all the progress we have made within. This is because the progress we make within is an expression of our behavior displayed to others through our lives. Your position in life is designed to strengthen your soul so that your life can constantly be fresh and new. When you become aware and remain focused on the drive and the direction of your life, you will change your world.

Therefore,
Work to solidify your position in life.
Work to fulfill any of the obligations you have
to your self and to your society.
Remain true to your self in all things
and never allow ego or self-interest lure you
into the direction taken by the outer world.

When you pray each day for direction,
you follow the path of rightness.
This path is easy to find
but difficult to follow,
for you will see many things
that will attempt to distract you.
Do not allow these distractions to influence your life.
Do not allow others to influence your soul.
For if you walk with confidence throughout your life,
you will become at peace.

Somewhere along your path you will notice the need for love. Somewhere along your path you will see people being treated poorly and will find it necessary to speak out. This awareness is the Spirit within you challenging you to grow. Allow this growth to occur for it will tell you that you are free and loved by your Creator.

Remember,
your strength comes from Spirit.
Your source is the Spirit within.

When you allow the Spirit to direct your life
it will take on a new and vital role.
You will become energized
and begin to challenge others.
Then,
the energy you obtain will bring you
into a different level of reality
and will change your life forever.

Welcome the changes
and challenges you will find along your road
and encourage your soul to express itself in your life.
Then,
follow the advice given by your soul
and accept the peace it offers.

Your life will change as you follow your soul's path.
You will become at peace with the changes you see
and will work toward the completion of your soul's task
on this plane.

Realize that we exist on many planes during our lives
and that each of these planes serves and exists because of
the other. Do not become dismayed if each plane causes
itself to be noticed at different times during life. When we
work each plane with deliberation and plan our lives so
that they are visible, we will not feel uncomfortable with
them. We will discover that they are created by the Spirit to
allow us to gain the knowledge necessary to live a life free
of pain. That is, if we choose this path.

Choose life and freedom.
Choose to follow the spiritual path.
Listen for the news of the Spirit that lies within your soul
so that you will live
and walk in peace.

Our Creator sends messengers to help us in life so that the world in which we live can be easily approached and understood. Through these messengers, we can realize the Spirit's presence, we can achieve transformation in our lives, and we can accomplish all things the Spirit presents to us. We will see our position in life with clarity and will not fear anything that may come into our lives. As a child of the Spirit, you are given all the tools needed to succeed. Therefore, use the messengers sent to enhance your growth, and then, welcome their presence into your life.

Protect your soul from the materialism and negativity of this plane. Transcend this plane with peace and calmness and know that you are consciously making your choice in direction. Know that it is by this choice that you will determine the growth that will occur in your life. By willingly making this choice, you will be at peace with your decisions and will continue your walk forward through life. You will become happy, and will realize that your needs are being fulfilled.

When I walk within the Light, I know that while in this Light I am without fear. I gather strength, welcome the knowledge of the universe that I uncover, and because of this, remove worry from my life. When I move in the direction of my soul, I become content beyond my present beliefs and see that my future will depend on my honest intentions. Therefore, search onward in your quest through life and walk on your path without fear, for you will be given spirits and guides who will walk with you into the Light. You will enter their realms and cease wondering over the peace that is provided to you by the Spirit. You will act swiftly on the direction and needs of your day. You will become refreshed, will enlist others in your journey, and will tell them of the love you have found within. By doing this, they will know by example that it is through love that they will be able to move any obstacles they encounter in life.

Start to become a beacon of Light for others. Through your actions you will tell others of your love, for love is the ingredient that many lack in their lives. You will show them that by understanding the Spirit's love they will uncover the keys to the unknown. You will signal to them all the love that is found within your soul and will cause them to subconsciously gravitate toward its Light. Each of you, in this manner, can become a beacon of Light to others; and will affect all around you.

Share your life with others and become freed from the obstacles and bindings that are present within your life. By doing this, you encourage your self to become all that it can be. By helping others to understand their spiritual nature, their philosophies will change and in this manner you will cause an alteration in the polarity of this world. By reversing this polarity, a fundamental change will occur in the course of events on this plane.

If we look carefully at our lives, we will see that we already cause changes to occur within it. By committing to the quest for spirituality, changes will occur in our lives that will astound us. I notice how I lose focus without moments of quiet. I see how difficult it is to center my life when I am not communicating with my inner self. I realize it takes work to keep the channel open to my higher self and work to listen to the news given by my soul. It is through these things that great shifts occur in my life and in my life's perspective.

Each of us sees the world in our individual and unique way. By constant attention to the details of our spiritual lives, we can change our focus and thus change its effect on our lives. Simply watch your life closely and listen to your soul's voice. When you do this, you are putting time into

life and you will obtain results that are profoundly different from those who fail to take this necessary time. This
will allow you to walk through life with all the love that is
within your soul and will allow others to see who you really are.

I began to work with others to become stronger in my
faith. I secured within my self the knowledge of the Spirit's
power and love which is the real story and need of our world.
You see, your life's journey is the route you take to find the
Spirit's love. Begin to love all you contact and embrace the
ability you have to help them on their journeys, for helping
others is the greatest accomplishment in life.

We allow the events of our past to hinder us and need
to let them go. By doing this, we become ourselves and
change our world. Respond to the concerns of life by showing love. Respond by becoming who you are and by changing your mind's thoughts so that you will learn to grasp
these inner changes as real.

You are happy.
You are kind.
You are the things that all
would like to see in their world.

You see,
it is all right to be perplexed.
It is all right to be questioning
the real direction in your life,
for when you look from the outside,
you will see that you are moving
in the direction of your path.

It is necessary for me to believe in my self, in the abilities I possess, and that with this belief I can succeed in my
life. I also believe that I am here on this plane for purposes
which form my path. I find that spirits are present to help
with my direction and to see that I do not become side-

tracked by the events of my life. It is my responsibility to learn from my past and undo any of the mistakes I make so that I may alter my world. When I see this truth in the events of my life, I realize that when people misplace their thoughts of love they start to forget this help and begin to create problems in their lives.

This is what it takes.
The answer is simple.

Work hard each day
and relax each evening.

Take the time to ease
and center your thoughts.
Center and focus your life,
In doing this,
you will stop your self
from being deflected from your path.

Be yourself.
Let others be themselves
and let them travel their path.
Let them pick and choose their course,
watch them as they travel,
but stay within your self and be free.

You should follow the inner feelings and teachings presented to you by your soul. You need to look carefully to uncover any sadness that is within and replace it with joy. Notice how your path encourages others to become all they can be while they travel along their paths. This knowledge helps them become who they truly are.

Watch the world change around you.
Watch it hover over the needs you have
for you are traveling in a direct line along your path.

It is necessary to look from the outside
to see your true movement.
It is necessary for you to work hard without fear
for the Spirit is always present
and will help you move onward.

Commit your self to the ideals
contained within your soul.
Commit your self to the spiritual path you follow.
Then,
follow this path as prescribed in your life.
By doing this,
you begin the life given to you anew.
You will respect your place on this plane
for you are placed here to accomplish
many goals and objectives.

By diligently following your inner voice
you will find and uncover your goals.
By fulfilling them,
you will be able to progress onward on your path.

The path we each take is the path to become whole. Each day of our lives is a new experience, allowing us new opportunities to accomplish our tasks and a new opening for the fulfillment of our visions. By following our paths, we learn to remember the needs of this life and begin to work on them with a passion. In doing this, we will not forget our accomplishments, the progress we have made in this life, or the search for the spiritual path we have undertaken, for it is on this path that true life is found.

The Spirit Within

What are we to find while we travel our paths? Where do they lead? I discovered the focus of my life was toward the Light and all its brilliance. I found that this Light directed me to its source, the Spirit within.

Seek the Spirit in all its goodness
for it is the correct direction to follow.
It will result in the most progress on your journey.

By denying the Spirit,
you will delay your becoming.
By pursuing it,
you will grow by leaps each moment you allow
its presence to be known.

Your quest in life is to become whole.
Your path is toward the Light.
Your needs are spiritual.
By traveling on this path,
you will climb higher,
and develop a peace within.
Remember your path as each day unfolds.

By doing this,
you will prevent discouragement.

You have seen
and will see fantastic moments in your life.
Learn to recognize them.
Learn to live from the feelings you uncover.
Do not forget them,
for when you present your feelings to others
you undertake the greatest leap possible in your growth.

All the things in our lives that cause us to become greater than we are, are found in the Spirit. The spiritual path is the essence of the human soul, for the Spirit created us in its image. Our soul is the image and reflection of the Spirit and is the greatest aspect of the human experience.

It is our free will that separates us from other species. Celebrate our free will, because by accepting Spirit into our lives we make the finest choice possible. Other species cannot make this choice and travel each moment of their lives by blind instinct. The choice to become or to wither is the greatest gift we are given. It is given to us so that we may become all we can be. Therefore, welcome this ability into your life for you will find that by using the free-will mechanism your choices will have great meaning.

Choose the spiritual way of life. It is the fastest road to the Spirit; however, it is also the most difficult. I found pain and despair are markers along this road and that I suffer and worry each moment that I hesitate to move forward along the path. Pain and despair may cause some to move more slowly on their path than they should.

Travel the correct path in your life
and remember the love that the Spirit has for you.
This fact alone will remove the pain.
Once a choice is made
you set the rest of your life into motion.

Growth toward the Spirit is natural,
it is effortless,
and without pain.
This alone will help you grow
and become whole.

Dwell upon the Spirit's love
and seek its presence in your life.
Allow peace to enter each day.
When you do,
you will grow in the Spirit
and obtain the peace you desire.

This is your purpose on earth.

Through the Spirit comes love.
Without the Spirit,
there is despair.
Walk not in despair,
but in Light
and become free.
Then,
take the time necessary to maintain that freedom
and work diligently toward its presence in your life.

Make sure you pause, reflect and empty your mind of the stress that accumulates each day. By taking the time necessary to do these things you will become happy, pain free, and you will think with clarity to become at peace.

Forget the past with its complications.
Today is a new beginning.
Tomorrow will make the change.
Begin to learn to encourage your self daily
and watch the progress you will make.

Begin to welcome tomorrow's challenges,
remember who you are,
and hear your self speak.

Light Seeds

1. How does change affect your world? List 5 ways.
2. List 5 ways the Spirit has touched your life. How has it challenged you to grow?
3. Have you noticed guides and messengers in your life? What have they said to you?
4. How do you know when you are walking in the Light? List 5 ways.
5. How does the Spirit direct your life? List 5 ways.

6

Inner Work

"No life ever grows great until it is focused,
dedicated and disciplined."

Author Unknown

How many people have you met who feel that they are given all the tools necessary to survive in life? How many forget that they have a role in developing their soul's journey? How many fail to see that work is necessary to grow? It is important to realize that your life's journey involves work to uncover its path. It also requires work to develop this path and to use it to aid others. I discovered that the way I expressed this work in my life was the result of the effort I put into my life.

Within each of us
is the real stuff of the universe.
Within us is the secret given to man by the Spirit,
the jewel of greatest price,
and the true reflection of the Creator.
So,
be calm and know that it is good.
Be still and listen to the small whisper of eternity
that is within.

Opportunities will present themselves throughout our lives which will permit us to celebrate in our hearts the joy given to us by our Creator. It is important that we focus our thoughts on this joy and begin to become at peace with its presence. We can experience the lightness which peace brings and feel the richness of our life's experience by learning to seek the real self within. Finding the self permits us to become fulfilled and at peace.

Always seek that place within that is quiet.
Always seek the peace which only stillness can find.
Comfort your self by seeking within
the place where the Spirit dwells.

We can live each day to its fullest by walking hand in hand with our Creator and thereby continue our climb toward the spiritual blessings that are present for all to find. We can renew within our selves the Spirit's presence so we can continue to grow along our life's journey. Once we reveal its presence in our lives, we can expect great things to unfold and we will feel ourselves grow within its love.

I find it important to step aside and let the voices I hear speak clearly from within my soul. I do not prevent the reception of their news or stand in the way of their entry into my life. I simply work to obtain the peace and contentment they provide and listen carefully to them as I travel along my path. I study and remember any lessons that I receive until I understand them fully. By doing this, I find that as I travel within my soul and interpret its lessons I succeed more in my life.

Flow freely
and be a river of calm.
Flow without restrictions
and without divergence.

Flow evenly,
without ripples.

In doing this,
you will work to smooth out the bumps in life
and begin to travel free.

I gain much when I reflect on the activities of my day. I watch closely those things that do not seem to work and simply work to correct them. I use each opportunity given to me to eliminate any interference. This allows me to use each opportunity in my life to correct the failings of my past. I learn to become diligent in my life's work and schedule the moments of my life so I can be in peace.

Begin to watch how things fall into place.
See the improvement you make along your journey.

Then,
learn to be patient and strong.

Stand,
walk,
and speak in the Light.

Do not become angry.
Learn to prevent frustration
and disappointment in your life.
Thus,
you will allow your thoughts to flow freely
and will remove any bonds from the past.

Worship

Over the years I have spent quite a lot of time looking at how people worship Spirit. Many define worship in ways that cause constriction and pain. They prevent the growth that worship provides. What is necessary, is to look at worship not as an act, but as a state of mind that allows the Spirit to enter.

Worship began many years ago during earlier developmental stages of society. It underwent many changes as people added regulations and devised schemes to limit others' freedom to worship. Today, many believe in strict codes. Look carefully at these people and you will see that they are prisoners of their own design.

You see,
to be free is to worship the Spirit in all things.
To be at worship is to be at peace.
Therefore,
enter into worship
and allow your soul to become alive.

Worship in quiet
and in solitude.
For you will find that the Spirit is always waiting
and listening to your call.
When you become who you are,
you are in worship.
When you are in worship,
you encounter your soul.

Therefore,
take a moment
and think of the need for worship.
By worshiping
you will release any frustrations you find within
and free your self from bondage.

I try to walk each day within the Light of worship. Thus,
I rekindle within my soul the fire of love and contentment
and welcome into my life the new hope and Light I find.
Then, I travel slowly within my soul, learn to be patient,
and learn to follow closely the guidance I discover within
its depths.

Service to Others

An essential ingredient to living a successful life is being of service to others. That is, service to others without
thinking of our personal needs and wishes. If we take a
moment to wonder about the need for this kind of service,
we will begin to understand its importance in our lives.

Service is a quality few of us understand, but when we do, we become unselfish in our paths and become empowered to work with love and concern toward others in any relationship we fashion. Therefore, permit your self to understand and listen to others. Learn to relate to their needs and you will learn much from them. It will cause you to open your heart to the truth that all people contain and you will experience the joy of becoming. You see, success begins with service to others and continues with service to self. Everyone needs such service in their lives.

In providing service, I welcome others into my heart and open within it a place for all to meet. In my heart I can settle all the differences I may have with others, forget past moments that may have caused despair, and remain safe during any difficult passage in life. It is important to take time once within my heart, for I can alter my journey and thus alter the direction of my life.

Be pure and honest at all times
for without honesty only harm occurs.
Learn to love others as you would want them to love you
for this is the message you should hear loud and clear.
It is important to remember this lesson
and to place it foremost in your mind.

Pain

Pain is an emotion that most of us try to avoid through life. We work to prevent its development and rebel when it enters our lives. We wonder why it exists and try to understand its source. We feel that we could improve life by its absence and do not realize the benefits of pain, the lessons of pain, the reasons for pain. When I look at pain as a tool, I see it in a different light. I see it as an experience that teaches and adds value to life. I see pain as the result of improper thought and find it occurring when I want things in my life that are impossible to obtain. Pain is the result of walking the wrong path, thinking the wrong thoughts, or dwelling on the wrong issues.

Your task in life is to
walk quietly without fear along your path.
Walk slowly
and enjoy the thoughts you have.
Learn to focus on the Spirit's love and compassion.
Then,
begin to focus on the need for this love
and see changes occur around you.
Thus,
you will begin to plant the seeds of love
and caring in your world.

By doing these things, pain becomes lifted from the mind. When we give time to developing peace in our minds, we enjoy the inner peace we create. You see, inner peace equals a lack of pain and is a natural state of life. Pain occurs only when we forget the real needs of life and focus on the material things of this world. Focusing on things such as materialism, greed, social climbing, and dishonesty leads to pain. By focusing on honesty, love, caring, and peace, we find a lack of pain in our lives.

Enjoy every moment of peace given to you.
Enjoy every morsel of goodness in your life.
Give love
and receive peace in return.

When you endure hardships,
you will uncover the Spirit's love
and find peace within.

When you deny pain,
you fool your self.

Do not be a fool,
be at peace.

Endurance

I can't tell you how many times I have awakened from my conscious sleep feeling that I was unable to endure life's setbacks. I even took time to consider my path and came up discouraged. I wondered what quality of consciousness changed my perspective and allowed me to continue on my journey. I discovered that it was the ability to endure which allowed me to continue in my growth. Endurance is necessary to love. Accept those times in which peace is not present in life. You see, real peace exists within our being when we can endure the many trials of life. Enduring trials results in the development of inner peace and a world outside that contains the qualities of love and compassion. Learn to endure the trials of life and obtain a power that allows forward movement along your path.

These things are the basis for health
and well-being.
You are to
love,
care,
and have endurance.

Life's Journey

Our purpose on this plane is to show the love and caring found within our hearts to others. It is to be all that we can be without needing to show who or what we are to others, because what we are will show itself without fanfare or celebration. All who come near us will notice who we are, for being ourselves is the best way to ensure the continued presence of the Creator within our being. It is this presence that is needed to live the fullest life.

Some fundamental changes are necessary in order for us to undertake our role in this world. It is necessary to speak of the peace found within our souls to those around us. Then, it is necessary for us to grow in the direction of our dreams. Because it is our dreams that make the future happen and without them we would not be able to grow or develop our minds.

How many times have you wondered or become concerned over the life you lead? Are you seeking your highest goals in life? Are you reaching for the most you can achieve? Think about this for a moment. If we do not seek our highest goals, how can we progress onward? Without progressing onward, how can we succeed? Know that you cannot fail if you continually strive for the results you envision in your heart. Envisioning your goals allows you to overcome any shortcomings you may have. Actively thinking of your goals allows you to overcome the barriers you experience in your life.

How do you overcome these barriers? How do you develop the skills necessary to move onward? By searching we discover the skills in each person we meet. All that is necessary to manifest these skills is to uncover them. When we uncover them, they will shine and extend beyond our present state of being and they will be seen by all.

When you discover your skills
you will make each day a testimony to the Spirit's love.

You will make each day glorious
and fashion each day into a string of beads.
You can make them cheap pearls
or rare gems,
the choice is up to you.

With steady work and the constant help of the Spirit you can overcome any obstacle present in your life. You can witness the changes caused by your thoughts and imagine the highest goals possible in your life. Just do not let these thoughts go from your mind once you envision them, for by holding them in your consciousness will you obtain your goals.

> Always look toward the picture you envision
> and uncover new paths to follow.
> By searching diligently in your life
> you will find boundless joy.
> You see,
> finding is the fun of life.

Too many find by trial and error. Few deliberately set out to center their lives. They wander and lose the focus of their world. They strive and uncover a path to their greatest desires. It is important to realize that once you find your desire you must work to maintain your focus. Once you become what you desire, you will find it is also necessary to continue to think of your life's journey. If we fail to maintain the focus on our lives, it will fade, for the constant change and love caused by this focus is what allows us to progress onward on our paths. We can succeed in our life's quest. We can find the answers to our questions of life when we seek them with a passion.

Welcome the days when you become discouraged, because in them you will be able to see a contrast with days when Light is present. Knowing this contrast allows you to become steady in your course through life. When you become steadfast in your love for all humankind, you will find prosperity and will not turn back on your journey, but you will continue securely on your path.

> Wonder at the miracle the Creator has made
> by giving you life.
> Appreciate the thought that you can witness its presence.
> Celebrate this news
> and welcome the fresh start that each day brings

to become at peace.

Remember,
each day is a new beginning,
each new beginning is a miracle in blossom.

When we undertake the path of the Creator in our lives, we uncover the good found in all humankind. We will not dwell upon the negative aspects of life, but will open our hearts to all we see and become amazed at the changes we can make in their lives. When we show love to all we meet, we will welcome love into our hearts and change the very fiber of our being.

The Gift of Touch

Take a moment from your reading and wonder about the gift of touch. Take a moment and think of our ability to touch a flower in bloom. In doing this, we witness the Spirit's goodness in our lives by celebrating our ability to touch a piece of its handiwork. Spiritual beings cannot explore as we can. They cannot feel the touch of another and cannot experience the joy of a moment's caress. Only we can witness this miracle. Therefore, enjoy your ability to touch others and feel the joy that a touch can bring. Then, touch your self with love and kindness.

When we walk through life with this touch of wonder, we expand our ability to touch the soul of another. Accept the blessings you will uncover and begin to touch your own inner soul to become at peace. You will find the intimacy of touching and you will realize that being without the touch of love is to be without life.

Enter into all things with love
and continue toward your goals with a touch of kindness.
You cannot touch your way
without finding the Spirit's presence within it.

Begin to walk alone
and find calm.
Begin to walk within your soul
and become understanding.
Finally,
walk gently as you pass through life
and learn to become at peace.

Do not worry whether you can see the areas in your life that need work. Seeing is a special gift for those who have undertaken the journey into the Light. Looking within is the most difficult of tasks, for it takes time to look within. It is unfortunate that few are willing to spend this time or are willing to accomplish this quest in their lives.

Therefore,
go onward along your path
and know that the Spirit's peace is within.
Go onward as you travel in life
and learn to be at peace.

By doing this,
you will welcome each new day you find
and will seek to love each person you meet.
When you do,
you will spread joy throughout your life
and will walk within this joy.

The Need to Win

How many people do you know who spend time worrying about who will win or who will lose in life? How many stop their development by expending too much of their energies pursuing this goal? I found that to live a full life I need to live each day without the desire to uncover who will win or who will lose. When I overcame the human need to win over others, I began to proceed without hesitation toward my vision.

It is not important whether we win or lose in life. What is important is that we provide a space within our lives for love to grow and flourish. If we love each person we meet with complete love, each of us will win in life. This is an important purpose in life. You see, everyone can win without others losing. Why should anyone lose when everyone can always win?

Through love
you can win in life.

Through love
you can become your best.

By winning,
you are able to give your love away.

By giving your love away,
you have succeeded in beginning a new life.

Welcome times when others win.
Enjoy the celebration
and the peace winning brings to life.

You see,
many of you think you must win in life to succeed
when in reality
you win by being the best you can be.

Listen for the whisper of love others send your way,
work to begin a new life based on love,
and give your love away.

You also win
when you accept love
and compassion from another.

Since we project our presence to others each day, it is what we project to them that is important. This presence is important because it allows each of us to show our self; for what we show of our selves to others will determine what they will give to us in return. Therefore, start to absorb love and nestle it within your heart. In doing this, you will become pleased each moment you give that love away.

Inner Dreams

I've always had questions about the value of dreams. Many of my friends rely greatly upon the visions that dreams bring to them. They spend hours dissecting each moment and derive guidance and wisdom from each event they contain. They create dream journals and collect volumes of information that they use to change their lives. Is there a value to dreams? Are they useful in our lives? What do they show our conscious mind?

Dreams tell us of our soul's needs, for they open our minds to the arenas of life that our souls wish us to see. They are opportunities to show the conscious mind the inner workings of our souls. So, listen carefully to them since they are a direct channel to the inner workings of our minds. Observe them as an outsider since they will be an exaggeration of the direction we travel. If our dreams do not conform to the desires of our lives, look at them to see where they differ. Through dreams we will discover the areas in life that need attention so that we can continue our growth to its fullest potential.

Once you begin to seek the help of dreams,
you will notice a vast improvement
in the direction of your life.

Once you listen to their help,
you will see the direction of your life change.

Once the direction of your life changes,
you will see the world about you also change.

Intention

Since we create our world, we should create one in which we would love to live. The world within each of us is perfect, just, and without shortcomings. Imperfections are produced by altering our mind's image of the soul's message which our conscious mind receives. If we take the time to accurately interpret the images of our souls, we will see our life's direction unfold perfectly.

It is important that you send a proclamation to the universe of your intention to change your viewpoint toward your spiritual life. Tell it of your intention to live according to the universal truths you hear. Tell it of your intention to change the ways you communicate with others and of your desire to obtain peace within. This will mark the turning point of your life. This one declaration to the universe will allow you to alter your course toward the spiritual and to become the most you can be. You may see your conscious mind rebel at such a declaration. However, it is up to each of you to believe that you can make this change so that you can concentrate on the spiritual matters of the universe for the remainder of your life.

Spend the time necessary in quiet contemplation.
Spend the time necessary to understand your path fully
and to feel comfortable with your course.
Walk with your guides
and see beauty surrounding you.

Too many people talk about spirituality in their lives but do not live by spiritual principles. This is because the principles of this path are, at best, difficult to follow. How many people spread love to others? How many know the feelings of peace and contentment? How many are free from the pain of despair? How many are non-materialistic? Think about these things and remember the beauty within those who choose the spiritual path. Perhaps you wish to have more in life or perhaps growth is not happening fast enough for your satisfaction. Do not become disillusioned. If you are working hard on the direction of your soul, you will obtain what you desire.

> Walk only the path to peace and forgiveness.
> Walk only the path that leads to the universe.
> If you can,
> you will live your life to lead others
> on the path toward the Light.

Light

Have you ever been told about the effects that the Spirit's Light can have on your life? Do you understand its needs and the origin of its gifts? Let's take a moment to explore this Light and to realize what it can do in our lives. By living and being within this Light, I uncovered the greatest consciousness possible. I discovered how the Light from the Spirit is remarkably refreshing and clean. I saw how it energized me and allowed me to think clearly.

How do you feel while in this Light? Do you realize that your Creator's thoughts form this Light? Begin to internalize this Light, for it will transform your life and cause it to become fresh and alive. This Light has been present since the beginnings, is the purest distillation of the Spirit within, and transports itself to all creatures in the universe.

> The Spirit's Light is
> health,
> wealth,
> power,
> courage,
> strength,

patience,
perseverance,
love,
protection,
armor,
peace,
friendship,
care,
bliss,
wholeness,
and kindness.
This Light is all that you could hope to become.
Therefore,
receive this Light through love
and bathe in this Light to become free.

I found that Spirit is Light in all its brilliance. When I breathe the Light within, I discover a healing power and see how it exists to nourish me fully. Watch and see the miracles it creates on your journey during the quiet times of meditation.

Live each moment within the rays of this Light
and fill each day with its joy and fulfillment.
Remember this joy
and the feelings it provides.
Then,
attempt to show another its way.
By doing this,
you will grow in Spirit
and become a changed soul.

Make the effort to change your life. Do this by taking time to see the Light and to discover quiet times in your life. In these quiet times you will find that fellowship is the answer to loneliness, and you will learn to undo many of the hardships you uncover.

Remove all the barriers you see to peace and calm.
Rejoice in the news that you discover
and begin to heal the wounds of yesterday.
When you remove all the doubts from your vocabulary
you will see only goodness and grace.

Tap into the Light of your Creator
and find a resource and guide.
This will allow you to travel to worlds
undreamed of in the past.

You see,
when you begin to worship this Light,
you will see its face shine forth in your life.

How often do you feel like your life is out of phase or
that you cannot find direction? You search and yearn for a
beacon to follow. During times like these you need to find
a source of direction, a source of power. By taking the time
to quiet your life you will begin to discover a source, a
beacon, a marker for your life's journey. When you center
and focus your life, you will begin to realize a Light of
peace, a Light of joy, a Light of calm amid life's storms.
You will begin a quest to understand the Light, to communicate with it, and to wonder as to its origin. You will begin
to feel its love.

This Light you seek is the Light of your Creator. It has
been present since the beginning of all that is and will be
present for all of eternity. Search to find this Light and to
reach its source. Once contact is made, realize that this Light
will surround you for as long as you desire. Discover how
to enter this Light so you may cause all things in your world
to change. Within this Light, you become one with your
Creator and you grow to heights you thought impossible
before. You will find that what makes up this Light is the
pure energy of love.

When I enter into its brilliance I do not fear enemies

nor events that I encounter. I notice that when the Light is around me, I succeed in all the endeavors of my life and begin to welcome each day as a new experience to enjoy. While in the Light, I do not allow my self to become discouraged or dismayed, for I know that the Spirit is present in my life and protects me from all harm. I learn to forgive others when disharmony occurs and to forgive my self when I perceive any disharmony with others. I understand that love will endure these struggles when the Spirit's interests are at the center of my life.

We have this to learn:
Our Creator has come to us in many ways
and is within each of us.
We are the temple of its thoughts.

Free will is given to us
to fulfill our needs and desires.
Therefore,
walk within its Light.
Do not stumble or fall
for our Creator is with us always.

Follow the feelings and thoughts
you encounter in this Light.
By doing this,
you will discover the true way
and the true direction to follow in life.

Light Seeds

1. In what way does the effort you put into your life affect your growth?
2. What opportunities have you seen that allow the Creator's joy to manifest in your life?
3. Why does it take work to succeed in life?
4. Do you take the time to review your day to see areas when

change could have helped you to remain focused on your journey?

5. How do you define worship? When do you worship? How do you worship?

6. List 5 ways to serve others' needs.

7. How does service affect your life?

8. List 5 activities that produce pain in your life. List 5 ways to eliminate this pain.

9. How does endurance affect your world? Can you endure? How?

10. What goals are you seeking in your life? What is preventing you from achieving them?

11. How can you touch another's life to provide direction and guidance? Has your life been touched by another. How? When?

12 Do you feel that it is necessary to win over others? Can you live without winning?

13. What are your dreams telling you? How do they relate to the reality you see around you?

14. Can you make an intention to change your world? How? When?

15. How has the Light entered your life? List 5 ways. Do you see this Light changing your world?

7

Inner Mind

"First keep the peace within yourself,
then you can also bring peace to others."

Thomas A. Kempis

Let's take an imaginary journey to another time, another place. Don't worry or become concerned as we leave the familiar behind. We will travel to a location far from our present reality. It has neither time nor space. We can't find it consciously because it is beyond our realm of knowledge. It is a place where peace abounds and hatred or the fear of others is not found. This world is not of the physical nor is it bounded by physical limitations. It is a world free of distractions. Can you imagine such a world?

Such a world is difficult to imagine because of the training of our minds. It is necessary for us to free up the boundaries of our imagination to understand this world and to see the Light it contains. Take a moment to bask in its brilliance. Do you find the quiet strange? It is strange here because giving and receiving love is the basis of life. It is important to see this world, for this is the world in which Spirit lives. Here, you will sense the release of everyday frustrations and will notice a strong energy flow. Take a moment and imagine this type of world in your life. Wouldn't that change your overall reason for living?

Listen to the words you hear from this world.

Then,
embrace all you encounter with love.

In doing so,
you will become at peace.

In the spiritual world you hear, see, feel and touch by thought. You work, play, teach and learn by listening to those about you. There are no secrets or unknown desires. There is only peace and plenty. Imagine yourself in such a world. Imagine that we could have a world of this quality about us. Then, begin to see this world and begin to structure some of its elements into your life. By doing this, you will help overcome any boundaries set before you. Your future awaits you. Even though we are physical beings and must work within the boundaries set up by physical laws, our spiritual guides will help us cross over these boundaries into the universe of peace.

You are
so that you may become.

You live
so that you may grow.

You are here
so you may learn and develop.

You are your Creator's image
and it is good.

Therefore,
clear your mind of any wandering thoughts
purge it with the conscience of your soul.

By doing this,
you will encourage your life
by listening to the Spirit within.

We must learn to deal with the complex nature of our minds and egos. We must let down the boundaries of this ego and begin to live and develop the soul within. Once in touch with this soul, we will unfold the true nature of our being.

Work to enlighten your conscious mind.
Enlighten your every word and thought
for it is a beacon to others.

Use this beacon to broadcast good,
not as a vehicle of unkind thoughts.
For you are the flower of the universe;
you are the enlightened child of your Creator;
you are the one from whom all your creation has come.

Following the voices within allows me to see the wonder that the Spirit has made in my creation. I take the time to study the words given to me, surrender my mind to the goodness contained within them, and learn from them. Then, I remember that we are the Spirit's greatest gift.

You are the species the Spirit created
and are its children.
You are its true reflection.

Therefore,
you are needed,
loved,
and cherished.

Enrich your life by listening to that small voice within your soul. Listen carefully to this voice, for it will lead you toward your destiny. Listen intently and decipher the words you receive, for they will allow you to learn along your path by quietly seeking their advice and counsel. Listen intently to them, for in them you will find the answers to your dreams.

We should be proud of our accomplishments. However, we should not let this pride hide the joy we find within when we realize the real self which can take hold in our lives. We are complex beings. We simplify our complexity when we find and become our true selves, which is the reflection of our souls and the essence of our entire being. So, listen to your soul and become what the Spirit intends you to be.

Only through honest effort can we overcome the pull of this world—the desire of the human species to have all they can have, instead of being all they can be. Keep your priorities straight by realizing that we are working to grow, become and develop strengths as we add each lifetime to the next.

Feel the goodness contained within your soul.
Perceive the Spirit's voice through the song
that is heard within it.
Then,
freshen your life by encouraging your soul
to become whole.

You are your soul
and are made by your Creator
to enhance the soul's image.

Do not suffer,
for suffering is not the true image of the Spirit.
It is love,
joy,
and caring.
These are the real guideposts to follow.

You enrich your life by allowing your soul to mature. Listen to its words and focus on the real self that lies within it. Listen carefully to the direction that the Spirit has chosen for you to follow in your life, because it is when you welcome the Spirit's Will into your heart that you will bring continual peace into your being. Those who listen to this Will are rewarded with the peace of mind they seek.

Send only love to others.
Show them bliss and happiness
through this love.
It is your choice to change your world.

Peace of Mind

My life became full of wonder when I understood and
achieved peace of mind. Can you imagine the joy that is
derived from this peace? By focusing on the true purpose
of life I eliminated the distractions that limited my potential and which prevented me from knowing peace.

Your potential is unlimited.
Your potential is without bounds.
Only you limit your self
by not listening to your inner voice for the way.

Therefore,
listen carefully;
listen quietly.
Let all thoughts go from your mind
and allow the quiet to settle in.

Stop,
listen,
become still,
and see peace within.

Stop,
see,
and relish this moment of peace.

By doing this,
you move onward with a clear understanding
of the direction you are to take in life.

When I focus on the peace given to me by the Spirit, I find its presence in abundance. When I focus on the path I travel, I find myself moving forward in growth at an increasing speed. I thank those I meet in life, for through them I receive the greatest message about my life's journey. They act as a mirror and as a barometer of my life and give me warning if there is a need to search more within my soul. I receive inner peace when I look from their viewpoint and see that the direction I wish to pursue in my life is accomplished. Can you see, that without such help you would not see the truth of your direction?

Travel at a pace that is comfortable for you.
Travel with joy
and focus on peace as your goal,
for nothing in life comes without work.
Nothing in life is worthwhile
without changing your life and the life of others
toward the goodness of the Spirit within.

Grow,
expand,
enlarge your soul
and the Spirit within.
You will find that once space is made in your soul,
the Spirit will fill it quickly.

It is up to you to use each opportunity
to expand and grow,
to live,
to be free,
and to encourage others in their walk
to be at peace.

Each of us contains an eternal soul which determines the direction of our lives. Some choose to cover up the soul with accolades and material things, while others realize the importance of the soul and listen carefully to its guidance. Learn to do this, for by following this path you will see your self grow.

Learn to settle your differences within
and allow your soul to penetrate
all layers of your personality.

When you become saddened,
listen for your heart.

When you become quiet,
hear the echoes of your heart.

When you are alone,
center upon the love of the Spirit
and see the goodness that is within your soul.

Light Seeds

1. How would a world of peace affect your life?
2. Could such a world inspire you to greatness? How?
3. List 5 ways in which you are the Creator's greatest gift.
4. What ways are there to resist the pull of this world?
   List 3.
5. How can you feel abundance in your life?
6. How does your soul determine the direction of your life?

8

Inner Knowledge

*"The universe is full of magical things
just waiting for our wits to grow sharper."*

Author Unknown

Life's purpose is not a mystery. The means to discover that purpose is within each of us. All that is required is for us to take the time necessary to listen within to the knowledge placed there by the Spirit. Listen and hear the words that will allow you to move forward in your life because you are here to encourage growth on your planet. Growth becomes possible when we learn to trust our inner voice in all matters. This inner voice provides a means to communicate with the Creator of the universe and to learn about higher realms.

The connection with your inner voice
is present for your enrichment.
It is created to allow the Spirit's words to enter your soul.
It gives direction and guidance.
It gives peace of mind when needed
and will lead you into states of higher consciousness.

Welcome this small still voice and give it ample time to make itself known. Listen with intent to the words it speaks and take the time to learn each day the messages it provides. Through listening we remain grounded in the love of the universe. Those who do not take the time to listen to the inner voice will not hear its words of wisdom and will lose opportunities that the universe provides for growth. Take the time to listen and hear the words spoken by this voice. They will create joy and cause your path in life to open wider than ever before. Once your walk has begun, you will continue to follow the guidance given to you by this voice. You will find that without this guidance you will not be able to follow your path, will lose the means to eternity, and will lose the way to realizing your fullest potential.

Potential

The greatest gift we can give our Creator is that of our potential. It is the one thing that we are required to develop alone. It is deep within our being and is there without our conscious knowledge. Use your potential to its fullest, for if you use it for your enlightenment, the joy of the universe will be yours.

Read these words with care:

Your Creator has given you
all the abilities of the universe.
They are given without any thought of retrieval.
It is up to each of you to nurture this seed of love
and allow it to sprout
and grow within you.

The Spirit's love is within our being. It is present to show its goodness to others. Since you are in control of your destiny, do not waste your life but use all the tools at your disposal to grow. You have returned to this plane to grow, to seek the spiritual, and to help those who do not see the way to the Light.

Tap into the rich universe of knowledge
that surrounds you daily.
Use this knowledge to enlighten your world,
for it will result in an improvement
in all the patterns of your world and life.

Progress in the search for wisdom does not just happen; it must be sought. Therefore, uncover your inner wisdom, bring it to the surface, and discharge all the negative feelings you possess. This is the state in which all understanding occurs and is the way to higher levels of consciousness and inner peace.

Live your life in the peace
that only your Creator can bring.
Do this by walking the path that is guided by the Spirit.
Once you do,
you will find the knowledge needed in your life
and will watch your self grow.

Understand this knowledge of the universe
and listen carefully to the waves of energy
that will overtake you.
They will encourage you on your path
and will help you in your development.

While I walk the path that the Spirit has established for me, I look for markers to keep me on my path. I uncover a storehouse of knowledge and grow in proportion to the truth of my journey. As I grow through each level presented to me, I notice that I am receiving information that causes me to improve my path. Take the time each day to listen carefully to the information you receive, for it will guide you on your way.

Steadiness

Become steady in your life's work and move in the direction of your vision. Do not allow the circumstances of life to cause you to drift aside. Simply focus on the direction of your path so that you may move toward your vision without difficulty. If you allow your mind to wander, the original intent of your vision will not unfold in your life. That is why you must continually steady your mind through study and meditation to design a path to reach your goals.

Remain steady in your thoughts
and in your progression.
Remain steady on your quest.
Only through deliberate,
steady progression
can you hope to achieve your maximum potential.

Walk

I find it important to walk slowly along my path, for I do not arrive at my destination by large leaps of faith, but by slow and deliberate effort. The pace of this walk is different for each individual. Some are satisfied with a slow deliberate walk while others move swiftly and accurately toward their visions. For me, it is important that I move in a deliberate direction so I can prevent myself from becoming lost. You see, getting lost is as easy as forgetting to look where you have been or where you are going. When I keep my eyes on my vision, I do not stray from it easily. My path only becomes difficult to follow when I fail to deliberately place each step in front of the other. My path is easy for me to follow, because I commit to its completion and my mind focuses on the markers at the end of my journey.

Life, to me, is like a rainbow. Those who take the time to notice its presence see its beauty. Those who refuse to focus on its beauty see only color, but those who do, see the spectrum, complete and without flaw. Therefore, steady your path and look at the rainbow of life. See all the individual colors and realize how each has helped to make up the whole. Life is beautiful if you take the time to look and see how its components fit together to form a whole. Do not become trapped looking for the gold at the end of your walk, because you will miss the beauty of your journey.

Mark your course with joy and laughter.
Mark your life with moments of bliss
and days of love and laughter.

Through deliberate and determined action we will follow our paths to completion. When we come at last to rest upon the shores of our visions, we will know that our journey was worth every moment of work, joy, laughter, and sorrow. You see, we have the greatest potential of all the creatures present on this earth. Become thankful for this position in the universe, for the entire universe celebrates with us as we succeed in life. It takes a gentle touch to walk the path we have chosen, for we must walk this path with compassion and concern for others.

Look at your life and surroundings with an open mind. Do you see the world you wish or do you see a world that is foreign to the desires of your soul? If the desires of your soul are not present, alter your course and begin anew. You will stumble along the way at times, but this will happen even to the most earnest person. Just remember the reason for your being on this plane and focus on your journey. Think and confer with your soul and listen carefully to its input. The soul is in touch with the eternal and it can see and correct your path. Therefore, listen to its voice and be secure in knowing that the results of these deliberations will be in your best interest.

We are faced daily with the need for making decisions that were unknown to us moments before. The decisions we make will cause an alteration in our paths and could move us off our life's course. Because of this, it is important to check for the Spirit's teachings in our lives. We will hear these teachings in the murmurs given by our souls during the quiet times of life. At these times, we must listen, for all our guides and angels are waiting to have input into our life's course. Without this guidance and knowledge we cannot see our paths. No matter what direction we take, we cannot be sure whether danger or disaster awaits at any turn. With guidance, we instantly will see the effect our direction will have on our life's course.

Which way is best?
Which way will lead you to sure success?

The only possible answer is simple:

Follow your inner guidance daily.
Follow the wishes and desires of your soul.
By doing this,
you will use the quiet times of your life
to connect with the energy of creation
and clear the jungle of your mind.
Doing this
will allow you to obtain inner peace and calm.

In our present world it is rare to experience the calm and serenity that we need to direct our minds away from the quicksand around us. By having a clear vision of our paths, we have a clear idea of where we are headed. The bombardment of noise and interference that our minds receive daily from the world, removes the time and space for quiet and makes it difficult to realign our selves to our spiritual path. This allows our lives to continue in confusion and dismay. It is up to each of us to call upon our guides to touch the hand of the eternal so that we may obtain the energy necessary to continue in life. Then, we must use this energy to help us in our direction and on our paths.

Your life is created to move forward.
Each of you has your place and direction to go.
Know that the Light is the focus
and is the guidepost to follow.

Therefore, use your power and position in life to promote beauty around you. Focus clearly on the Light to become at peace, for when you steady your course in life and look toward the Light, you will fulfill your greatest potential.

You are responsible to follow through with your desire.
You are responsible for your destiny.
Therefore,
focus,
steady your course,
work hard and with diligence,
and your vision will become one of beauty and love.

Light Seeds

1. How do you discover your life's purpose?
2. List 5 ways you can bring your inner wisdom to your conscious mind's attention.
3. Why is it that you must remain steady in your life's journey? How do you accomplish this in your life?
4. How do you travel your path? Is it by leaps of faith or by deliberate action? Why?

9
Inner Growth

"Growth is the only evidence of life."

Cardinal John Henry Newman

I have spent many years studying my inner path and I realize that the most important result of my journey is the inner growth that I receive. As I grow, I interact with others in ways that I did not understand before. I am able to show compassion and to use it to heal the wounds that others have incurred through their lives. It allows me to see life differently, to react to situations I encounter with joy, and to permit joy to permeate my path. I enjoy a balance in life that provides a steady path and a constant source of nourishment.

Growth is the issue in life.
Peace is the issue in eternity.
Therefore,
live for the love in your heart
and the peace that is in your soul.

When you work to achieve this balance,
all else will be given to you.
Therefore,
work to spread love and caring.

Work to be kind.
Work to be pure.
Work to show the Spirit's love in your life
and you will find the peace of eternity within your soul.

Once the Spirit touched my life, I stopped searching for the peace I needed. I listened to my inner voice for guidance and realized the uniqueness of each day. I saw today as a gift given to me by the Spirit to use as I wished. I saw today as one of a limited number that I would have the privilege to see. I learned to use each day to cause good to happen to those around me and to use the time given to me to effect a change within my world.

Consistency

How many people do you know who live lives full of inconsistencies? One day is full of expectation while the next is one of dread and fear. Part of becoming whole is to provide a space where consistency flourishes; another is to show our consistency to those we contact. It is important to share it with others because this will cause them to become aware of the inconsistencies within their lives. We need to develop consistency to allow our selves to grow in the direction of our dreams. Therefore, work each day to develop consistency in your life. Do this by talking to others in a way that promotes its development and thereby cause an increase in the consistency of your world. Become consistent. Live, eat, and breathe consistency. Work to awaken this trait in everyone, and see your world change.

Imagine a world in which all people are consistent and in which all try honestly to overcome any obstacles they place in their way. If we could do this, we would not settle for less in our world but would recognize the potential that is within each of us to create a new world. Be consistent and enlarge your world.

Learn to encourage others to encourage your self along your path. Remove any doubt from your mind of the life you lead because it will allow you to follow your inner voice to the success you seek. How many people spend time in preparation for growth? How many do you know who spend time learning from the spirits around them? Each soul has an equal opportunity to contribute to society and an equal opportunity to grow and develop. It is regretful that few accept the challenge to grow. Few leave the materialism of this world to live by faith and belief. Those who do are

never disappointed. They are champions of the knowledge
they uncover.

It takes courage to fight the battles for growth
that are necessary both within our beings
and in the outer world.

It takes courage to accept the teachings given
to follow through with a new life
and to settle all the differences within
to make room for the news
received daily from the Spirit.

Learn to respect all others
and love them as you love your self.
Learn to grow along with them
and do not be reluctant to grow against them.
Learn to realize that each of us grows at a speed
that is comfortable for us.

Thus,
learn to be gentle
and kind.
Learn to have patience.
Learn to develop skills that will allow you
to comfort others.
Learn to acknowledge your errors,
and by doing this,
grow each day.

You will grow exponentially each moment you allow
the Spirit's love to enter your life.
You will become greater within,
will grow to see goodness in all people,
and will grow each day that you possess
the power of the Spirit within.

Light Seeds

1. Why is growth the most important result of your life's journey?
2. List 5 inconsistencies in your life.
3. How can you become consistent in these areas?
4. How can encouraging others create consistency in your life?

10

Inner Tasks

"The race is not always to the swift,
but to those who keep on running."

Author Unknown

Wonder no longer over the course you are to take in life.
Simply seize it
and walk.

Walk in abundant peace.
Walk within the Light
and become changed.

Become all that your Creator created you to be
and accept with dignity the life created for you.

Learn to be your self.
Love your self.
Love others as the Creator loves you.
Love all parts of you so that you may become whole.

Your world will learn the need for love,
for your world is changing with rapid speed.
Unless people take time to know their selves,
there will not be hope for their happiness.

You see,
time is forever.
Happiness is now.

As we travel along our spiritual paths, we will find it
impossible to return to our previous ways of life. We will
become new and follow a different theme in our lives. This
difference is a gift from our Creator and is unlike any other

given to us. As we travel our paths, we must learn to keep our thoughts at their highest level to become awakened, for we are to walk within the footsteps of our Creator and learn great things. As our paths solidify, we will develop self-esteem and will remember that we are a reflection of the Spirit.

When you find it consciously difficult to travel in this new direction, think of the love you are given. Think of the direction in which you are heading, notice from the outside the direction you came from and where your are going. In this manner, you will see that you have made great strides in your life. Consider for a moment how your path has changed and see how much you have developed each day. You have been on this path for many lifetimes and may only now see the connection between its various events. Choose the correct path, for when you do, your future will be remarkable. Do not fail to make this choice, for you cannot leave your future up to chance. You cannot vacillate on the direction of your path as your path must become steady. You accomplish this by taking time to look at your direction as you walk along your path.

Learn to avoid any of your past mistakes. Look to your future and begin to travel toward your desires by visualizing the future you wish. Then steadily, little by little you can begin the walk toward those desires. Only by constant determined movement toward your desires will they become realized.

Become committed
and become determined.
Steadily,
daily,
walk your path.

Courageously set out upon your new course.
Steadily onward.
Steady as you go.

Constantly pursue your desires.
Constantly focus on the result.

It will happen!

People fail because they do not have determination and do not set their course through life. Be sure to set your sails with determination, for when you do, you will reach your shore and become what you envision.

This is the formula all should follow:

Keep your thoughts toward your vision.
Keep them constantly in view.
Remove any doubt about your course
and eliminate fear.
Eliminate thoughts or feelings of impossibility
and welcome each day as a new beginning.

Once this is accomplished
you will treat everyone as you wish to be treated
and will see unbelievable changes in your world.
You will uncover a vast storehouse of knowledge.
You will prosper,
grow,
and succeed.

Understanding the physical world is a difficult task. When I look around in my life, I see many things that cause confusion and dismay. I see how people don't always recognize things that permit spiritual advancement or even see them as causing harm to others. Often, beliefs and personalities enter the decision-making process and cloud the real issues all face in life. During these times I remember the diversity within the human population and remember the ego's need for superiority. Worldliness and materialism cause people to forget their paths and to focus on the wants,

not the needs of life. Focus on the needs and do not overin-
dulge in the wants. Doing this will cause the development
of a healthier, happier society in which to live.

The basics of life are simple:

Treat others as you would treat your self.

Learn to respect all life.

Begin to encourage each other to grow
and become kind to all you meet.
By doing this,
you will show love and compassion
to each person you meet.

What kind of thoughts enter your mind as you listen to
others speak? Instead of love, you hear envy, jealousy and
greed. It is no wonder that we find it difficult to remain
centered in this world. The time has come for us to look
upon others with love and to become gentle and kind to
them. We need to center our thoughts, focus on our needs,
and begin to love each person we meet. Others will follow
a path that is windy and dangerous and will place themselves on a collision course with their inner selves. They
will use the ego and forget the self. They will feed the ego
with words, forget humility, become unhappy, and will not
find peace. It is important to take time to learn from them,
avoid the same pitfalls, and to learn what not to do in our
lives. We can do this if we look and listen to the clues
shouted at us daily. If we simply envision the future and its
needs, we will discover the path we need to follow.

Never doubt your spiritual abilities.
Never fear the path you travel.
Only continue along your path without hesitation.

Then,
remember the changes you see
and the growth you have undergone.

When you see your growth,
you will be thankful for all that has taken place
in your life.

Travel,
enjoy,
and always be happy in your life.

Learn to walk in peace
and be kind to all you meet.

Learn from those you will see along your path
and enrich the lives of those whose lives you will alter.

The cost of following the spiritual path is to walk alone on your journey of love. Others will see you and wonder why you persevere but you must keep them from entering your innermost space. You must remember that the future is related to the now, the now is a reflection of your soul, and your soul is eternal. Simply walk in your soul's shadow and watch peace become your way.

When I take the time to contact my deepest desires and to think on things that cause me the greatest joy, I become my greatest. The things of this world cause me to become bitter and distressed, while the things of the eternal are the important ones to see. Therefore, concentrate upon the means to provide the Spirit's love to all who contact you. In doing this, you will become at peace, you will discover a new life, you will learn to follow the voices within, and you will become freed from the stagnation of the world about you. It is these things that will change the world you see.

Light Seeds

1. In what ways have you changed since you began the spiritual path? List 4.
2. Do you seek your goals and visions with determination or are you complacent in your growth?
3. List 4 areas of confusion in your life.
4. How can you find clarity in each of these areas?
5. In what ways has the spiritual path improved your journey? List 5.

11

Inner Sustenance

"The best [man] is like water.
Water is good; it benefits all things
and does not compete with them.
It dwells in [lowly] places that all disdain.
This is why it is so near Tao."

Lao-Tzu

I have seen many people in my career who have spent their lives achieving great material wealth. In each case, I have seen pain and sorrow behind the tired glow of their eyes. As time passes, the glow diminishes and is replaced with the dull glaze of sorrow, as they realize what they have missed during their mad rush to succeed. Material success has its price and that price is not worth the anguish it creates throughout life. You see, the external world is full of opportunities to grow and to become a leader in the realm of material gain. It is not equipped to allow us to translate this growth into our inner world. Because of this, a tug of war develops between the outer and inner worlds and prevents inner peace from being achieved. This split creates a separation that divides our minds and creates confusion. What we need to heal this split is to end this confusion and create wholeness in our lives.

Keeping the Spirit's love foremost in our minds allows us the means to become whole. Our ego personality will not disguise the real soul within, for the soul is created perfect. We continue to be in this perfect form but are in a body that sets many limitations upon us. By focusing on the Spirit, we overcome these limitations and are freed from the artificial boundaries we create.

Search your heart each day for your Creator's love and use it as you react and meet with others. Love is given to you freely and helps you to focus on your daily tasks. Do not underestimate this love, or the power that is within it, because it can lead you into the growth necessary to change your life.

> Allow the Spirit's Will to surface
> and follow its wishes.
> Uncover it
> and listen to the direction of your soul.

> Remember to stand firmly on its teachings
> and recall it in each new moment of your life.
> Your soul will instantly recognize the Spirit's Will
> and act upon its call.

> Happiness exists.
> The Spirit is the way.
> Therefore,
> encourage your self and others
> to seek and follow this truth.
> Then,
> welcome it within your life
> and celebrate the awakening of your soul.

The language we use when we speak to our selves is essential to amplify the growth that is taking place within. We should always listen, hear positive things, and train our inner ears to hear these moments of growth. Then, we need to report them to our conscious minds to aid our growth processes. This will amplify the goodness we find within and will show it to the outside world.

> Focus upon the Spirit as it works in your life.
> See its goodness
> and share it with others.

Nurturing

Before growth can occur, it is necessary to water and fertilize developing seedlings to provide the proper nourishment for life. In order for a child to mature into an adult, it is necessary to nurture it over time. This is also true of the Spirit. Nurturing is essential to our overall development. It is important to nurture the direction and way in which we travel and to nurture our minds with a positive flow of information. It is necessary to the overall success of our transformation, for when we learn to nurture our thoughts, we will become in harmony with our vision. We will then use the moments we have to focus on our paths and their needs to nurture the direction of our journey. This will cause us to grow in the direction of our dreams.

Work with the Spirit and the universe
to apply all the knowledge that the universe supplies.
Then,
study the people about you
and see the world that you are creating.

By nurturing your way,
you will create the reality you desire.
Then,
you will become at peace with your journey
and will allow the universe to direct your path.

Light Seeds

1. What is your attitude toward material success?
2. How has material success affected the lives of others you know?
3. Has it caused a separation in their world?
4. What can mend this separation? How?
5. List 4 ways you can nurture your soul.

12

Inner Steps

"We go through life as some tourists go through Europe
so anxious to see the next sight;
the next cathedral;
the next picture;
the next mountain peak;
that we never stop to fill our sense with the beauty of the present
one."

Minot J. Savage

The journey of which we all are a part, is the journey called life. To obtain the most from this journey, we must realize the need for constant growth and development. It is also necessary to travel in steps that will allow the incremental expansion of our world so that we can use the knowledge we gather to live our lives to the fullest. These steps allow us to learn through doing and to become teachers by allowing the essence of our lives to create our world.

I enter the quiet moments of each day with my mind set upon the peace given to me by my Creator. In studying this peace, I am able to recognize any crossroads I encounter in my life. I realize that I travel a path that allows me to see and to study the soul I truly am. I learn to center my thoughts on the goodness that surrounds me and to feel the peace that these thoughts bring. I discover guides who are present to help me in my transformation and with their help begin the process of change in my life. Each of us can welcome this aid and comfort into our lives. Once we allow this help, we will never again look for the old ways we lived, but will travel refreshed and strengthened by the wisdom we will encounter.

I am impressed with the realization that I have been working on my soul's development for many lifetimes. I do not need to rush to meet arbitrary deadlines or to complete the life cycles I am privileged to see. In fact, rushing through any cycle will only cause failure in my way. I know that I only need to uncover the maximum information available to me so that I will learn at a steady pace. Approaching my growth in this manner allows me to know that I will complete my present cycle of development at the proper time independent of my present frame of reference to time.

Living our lives to become all we can be is the best way to live. Thus, we work each day to improve our lives, if only by the slightest amount; and travel step by step, growing to higher and higher levels, until the final lessons we need are learned, absorbed, and taught. This completes our life's purpose: to learn all that is possible on this passage and to teach others what we have learned.

Teach by living,
not by speaking.

Teach by fulfilling your obligation to others.

Teach by example
and become a beacon of Light to others.

I speak to others with an open heart each opportunity I am given and show love to those I meet in my life. I undertake those things that are moral and live to transform my world into a showcase of love. I do this by talking to and understanding the people I meet each day. I discover how to avoid disaster in my life by correcting the obstacles to peace I uncover along my path. I do this before they develop into pain, eliminating them through communication and understanding.

Begin tomorrow to look for this new direction in your life. Start by noticing the world around you, then, state your intention to change the structure of your world. Begin by affecting those immediately around you, for they will quickly notice any changes you make in your world. As you continue to follow your road, you will influence an ever widening circle of people. They will eventually influence others and this cycle of influence with expand and grow. Thus, one soul can affect many, through an ever-expanding circle of influence, for we are all linked for eternity.

Thought

Did you know that you can change the reality of your world with a single thought? This is possible because thoughts do perform miracles as they form the essence of the universe we see. It is when we uncover our mind's thoughts that our lives will become enriched. We can still and direct our thoughts during times of quiet contemplation. Stillness allows the realignment of our souls and helps us to smooth our emotional needs in order for our entire being to rest. This will encourage us to see joy and happiness and to walk in an attitude of peace and contentment.

You can begin to direct your thoughts as you learn to study the causes of your reality and the interrelationships of others in your life. Understand that your mutual thoughts can change the direction of the reality you see. This is why Spirit has come to work with those who are willing to take the time to learn these lessons. Those who will listen, will begin to change the thought patterns of their world, and cause changes that will become increasingly profound as time progresses.

We begin each day with a single thought which is the seed that creates our entire day. Respect this thought and become comfortable with its meaning, for thought is the basis of hope. Thoughts are constantly available and determine the path that we travel. Our object is to learn to control our thoughts and to eliminate those that cause us harm. By correcting the harmful thoughts, we can change the direction of our lives and in turn cause a change in the life direction of all we meet. By centering and focusing on our good thoughts, we bring happiness into life. By thinking from our soul's perspective, we become a new person and are able to bring its contents to the surface of our mind. By living on the soul level we create vibrations in the world around us and cause a change in the reality we see.

We live in a space created by our reality. It is possible to change that reality instantly. Create a reality of love, compassion, peace and forgiveness, and work each moment toward fashioning these qualities in your life. Enlighten your mind by looking and seeing the happiness that the Spirit provides. When you do, you will regain your viewpoint in life and grow in the direction of your dreams.

Life

We live in a time when many in different corners of our world do not value life. Few understand how fragile life is or see life as the loving creation it is meant to be. Cherish life because it is the most precious state in the universe. Life's purpose is to develop, grow, become great and achieve the highest level of growth possible. Enable your self to achieve this purpose by working from within to create the real image of your soul.

Your reality,
your very state of being,
is determined by your soul.

Uncover this jewel
and live your life in peace.

Become all you can be
and begin to grow daily in your Creator's service.

By learning this,
you have found a great secret of creation.

> Be pleased with your discovery
> and dwell within your soul.
>
> By living your soul's reality,
> you will actively change your world.

Inner Growth

Before I entered this plane, I created a vision of my world. As soon as the Spirit helped me see this vision my life began to change. I found it difficult to rest until I was able to develop this vision to its fullest potential. I saw others stop their development as they dropped out along the way because they made the choice to remain at their present stage of growth. They failed to realize their vision and stalled their development by losing track of their purpose in life.

The first step in anyone's growth is to realize that they are directed from within. Once this is discovered, they move rapidly forward in life. It is sad that many take lifetimes to discover this truth or fail to use this wisdom to obtain their inner guidance. Find this guidance within your soul and see how it gives you peace and joy. Discover this guidance and add true meaning and direction to your life.

> Look always to the Light for support and comfort.
> Travel through your life with the love found
> within your soul.
> By doing this,
> you allow others to see
> and will become amazed at the purity that fills your life.

Take the time that is needed to look around your world and see the difference you can make. Look and realize that the life you lead is the result of your conscious and unconscious thoughts.

Even in complexity,
simplicity reigns.
You are each responsible for the reality you project.
You continually influence those in your life
and cause both of your worlds to exist.

Each day is a new adventure.
Each day is a new beginning.
Each day is an opportunity to develop
in ways unknown to you.
Each day is an opportunity to visit the Spirit in your life.

Light Seeds

1. List 5 steps that have led to the expansion of your world.
2. Do you feel you are rushing through the cycles of your life? If so, how can you change this to learn each cycle fully?
3. List 5 ways you teach others in your life.
4. What thoughts do you have that could change your world? List 5.
5. In what way do these thoughts add value to life?
6. What is the first step in your growth?
7. What type of thoughts create your life? How do they change your reality?

13

Inner Walk

"If you find yourself further from God than you were yesterday, you can be sure who moved."

Author Unknown

Society has built many obstacles to understanding the true nature of humanity. It places external rewards and achievement as the goals to which all should aspire. This has replaced the real nature of life with outer needs. You see, part of changing the direction and potential of our lives is the movement of our attention inward to see the real nature of our souls. This change in direction requires an inner walk which must be taken alone; a walk that allows the realization of peace and the awakening of a new tomorrow in our lives. To do this, we must become like a child and look around us to find those things that will cause a difference in our world. We must look closely to discover outer changes that will occur because of the inner changes we make. We must stay on this inner path of change because practicing these inner changes will create a habit that will cause our world to open.

I affect my world each moment of my life. I set up vibrations that lead either to a renewal or a loss of life energy. I find it important to work to increase my life energy and to walk my new path, for once my path was found, I was able to travel upon it and grow continually. Look at the progress you can make in your life. Notice how you can grow if you focus and center your self and not lose control of your destiny.

Inner Source

Where is the source of your life found?
Who controls the engine that drives your life?

Where can you find the answers you desperately desire?

The answers are found along your walk in life. You are the source of your destinies, and by focusing on the direction of your life, all you need for the accomplishment of your path will emerge. When you walk along your path with confidence, you will realize that the resources you need will present themselves to you.

Think about situations that required special interventions.
Didn't they happen at the right moments?

Trust the Spirit within
and work with guides that are given to you.

Become your source
and be free from the pain of indecision.
For once you accept your position as source,
your world will drastically change.

I learn to be the source to my self and to continue on my path even when difficult times come my way. I know that life travels in cycles just as nature causes spring to follow winter. I realize that I am able to move forward without fear and to not settle for my present reality of life, but to use my life to provide learning experiences along my walk. I find the inner journey is the hardest journey of all. I see many who attempt to travel in the direction of their inner voice but fail when they find the amount of work that is necessary to pursue this course. They discover that it takes diligence to move on their path because success only occurs through effort. Those who feel that work is not necessary are the ones who will not find success. Those who realize that they create their own reality and are able to affect that reality in their lives, are the ones who will continue to grow and build their worlds.

Build yourself a world of beauty.
Build yourself a world of fun and joy.
You are responsible for your world
and are the source of it all.

When you think about changing your world,
you will cause it to change.

Don't be one of those who refuse to take the time to see their world as it is, and continue through life failing to see how they can affect its outcome. Don't neglect to see that by becoming the resource and source of your life, you will move toward your preferred future. Learn to be the source of your life and thus create rapid inner growth. Doing this will enable you to uncover the stagnation and loneliness that occurs when you fail to focus and center your mind. It is up to you to pursue the journey you have begun, to keep in touch with your soul, to continue to grow, to be at peace with your self, and to develop your soul daily. To become free, remember that the Spirit is the strength from which you derive your direction in life.

Rest secure in the path you travel.
Verify any thoughts that are in your mind
and know that they are good.
Then,
continue the path you have chosen
and walk within the Light to prosper.

We are spiritual beings on this earth. We are the embodiment of the Spirit and as such are the greatest creation known. Take time to ponder this fact and to unleash all the power that you find within your being. By finding your power, you will stop doubting your abilities, and with diligence and thought begin to study your way. Doing this will cause miracles to happen.

You are a child of the Spirit.
You can climb to great heights.
You are these things.
That is,
you are
if you believe.

Inner Spirit

As my world changed and grew, I found that my focus centered on the internal values that the Spirit provides. I studied, searched, and found the peace that this inner source gives. I then began to listen to its call and heeded its advice. I quietly listened and accepted my position and direction in life. I discovered that I could change my world with the thoughts I heard. All it took was being alert to the Spirit within.

Each of you must travel a road which you alone can navigate. You share the spirit realm with each other as each of you form a part of the great whole. While contributing to this whole, you are responsible for the thoughts brought out from your world. Your beliefs are nurtured from conception as your thoughts continually develop within. You bring these "programs" with you into adulthood and use them to develop your path. Welcome these programmed thoughts into your adulthood and recognize them for what each represents. Thus, you can alter their effects and modify your thought processes so that they are in keeping with the Spirit.

Become less fixed
and more open.

Become more at ease with thoughts
alien to your way of thinking.

By considering these thoughts,
you can alter your journey
and remain on the Spirit's path.

The Spirit is within you
and will guide you always.
Wonder about the Spirit and realize
how it reflects the true image of your Creator.

The level of growth we reach in life is directly related
to the degree of spirituality we allow ourselves to achieve.
We place a limit on our level of spirituality and thus alter
the course and complexity of our lives. By taking time to
dwell on the Spirit, we will become free and will expand
our growth potential. This expansion of potential is the
growth we seek.

Grow continually
by listening to your inner voice.
Listen carefully for the messages it brings
and use them to call upon its wisdom.
It is this wisdom that produces the greatest inner peace.

Worship the Spirit
and remember that it is the source of your self.
Dip into the lake of its love
to witness true peace.

As you travel, steady your path and enter the realm of
the Spirit. Use the events you see in your life to amplify
your growth and use the experiences you gain to fulfill and
further your path. This is the way to settle conflicts or differences you may discover within and to allow your self to
grow to its highest potential. Then, develop patience toward the events you see in your life and don't allow yourself to become bitter over the untimely events that may occur. Simply keep the thoughts of the Spirit within your heart

and remain at peace.

I look within my soul for strength. I look within it for the compassion, drive and the fulfillment of my needs. I do not need to look outside my life to find true happiness, for those external and material things will not provide any of the feelings given to me by the journey within.

Follow the self.
Listen to your inner voice.

You are to search for your spirituality
and for the truths given by your Creator.
By searching,
you will find that the reward for this journey
is unbelievable joy and happiness.

To receive this reward, I train my self to seek thoughts of happiness. I look on the positive side of events in my life for that is the path I find as quiet, peaceful and without fear. It is calm and serene.

So,
listen for a moment to your heart
and take the time to gather sunshine within your soul.

Allow it to expand to your friends
and loved ones.

Quietly listen
and seek the love within your soul.
Then,
tell others of this love.

I allow my mind to still before I enter times of quiet or dwell upon the goodness presented to me by the Spirit. Doing this leads me into the proper channel for the clear reception of its love. Let your Light shine onto others by giving them kindness, understanding, peace and love. Listen in return for the murmurs expressed in their hearts.

Learn to respect
and enjoy your times of quiet.

Learn to be.

Thank the Spirit for the abilities given to you and for the love you find in life. Thank your self for taking the time to listen to the Spirit and for living the life you presently lead. Once you do this, you will share your thoughts with others who are in need, and seed your relations with love. Be thankful for those you contact in life and thank them for the lessons they teach you. By becoming one in Spirit, you can alter history and contribute to society each moment of your life.

Therefore,
be peaceful,
be kind,
be thoughtful.
Communicate to each other the messages
given to you by the Spirit.
This alone will cause you to notice the spiritual life
you have undertaken.

The benefits of living a spiritual life are numerous. To see them, we must take the time to walk within and carefully look at our souls. This simple step will improve the quality of our lives and affect those around us. You see, wonderful things will happen to those around us because of the changes that will occur in our lives. We will notice a change in their attitude and posture, and will be able to continue forward along our paths to walk effortlessly within the Light.

Surround yourself with those who show compassion

and love, and continue forth with the knowledge of the inner direction given to you. Notice how you participate with others in your life and how you decide on the way that provides both peace and kindness. Have you found that road? Take a moment and ask your self about the road you presently travel and then think about the way you wish to spend your life. Some people spend their lives in frivolous pursuits while others spend their time creating the most productive world possible. By watching their way of life, you will learn much; for those around you are the best teachers in your life.

Look carefully at your self. What do you see? Do you see honesty and love? Do you see a way of life that best uses the time given to you to grow and develop? Using your thought process, you will focus all your attention on the real needs in your life. You will follow the guidance provided to you from the Spirit within and allow its gentle touch to caress your mind, thus leading it into the peace of eternity.

The Choice for Peace

I spend a great deal of time contemplating my inner world. I hear the Spirit and pay attention to the words it speaks. I see my direction in life with clarity and move forward knowing what path to follow. I realize that along the way opportunities will occur to change the direction of my world. I also know that choices will be required, for choices create my direction and thus create my world. What tools are available to help me make these choices? Where do I turn to see my direction? I use my resources to create a world of exceptional beauty and look at this beauty to discover the wonderful things my life represents.

Choose to make your life's path
one of love and caring.

Choose the path to joy.

By living within joy as the framework of your life,
you will dwell within happiness.

So,
clear your mind of all thoughts
and cleanse your life so the Spirit can enter.

Each of you makes the choice for this entrance to occur.
Each must live with the results of choosing otherwise.
Therefore,
make the result of your choice the best possible.
Make it the one that will encourage others on their paths.

Choices are difficult for some to make because to them
choice is a frightening thought. Some people fail to realize
that they are given the opportunity to choose and, therefore, have a difficult time steadying their course through
life. Learn to choose wisely by listening to the feelings you
have within. If you follow them, you could change all of
creation. By actively choosing, you will strengthen the
bonds between each other and will welcome the changes
you find within your being. Begin, therefore, to work each
day to increase your potential by consciously listening to
your inner voice for guidance. Then, choose to decide the
course you will take in life.

Choice is like a muscle. By constantly exercising the
choice mechanism, we develop strong abilities. When we
fail to develop this mechanism, it eventually weakens and
becomes lost to our conscious mind. We have the choice to
make our world change. So, choose to make the change to
move forward along your path, listen to your heart and soul
during times of quiet, and encourage others so that you will
become at peace with your self.

Look upon others with compassion and remember that
they have all the difficulties and complexities in their lives

as you do. They have hardships and pain and are attempting to create their own reality. Realize how necessary it is to control and live your reality. By using the soul's knowledge to direct your life, it will continually enlarge and give you great joy.

Therefore,
continue onward in the Spirit's love.
Continue to enlarge your world.
Continue to grow.
Continue to work with others
to create the world of your dreams.

It takes work to continue on your chosen path. See how others choose their paths. Notice how their paths differ and see how over time their paths may cross. Learn to use these crossroads to grow. Use them to expand your base of love and to create a paradise on earth. You can do this when you commit to joy, love, and peace in your life.

Peace is known by few in this world,
distress by the multitudes.

Begin to develop peace.
Learn to create peace
and you will be free.

Do not obstruct the peaceful way in your life,
but learn to define it,
work for it,
and pursue it.

The result will be a life filled with spiritual love.

When we encourage those about us,
we will allow our selves the time and space
to affect another's love.

When we give our love to them,
we find that love returning to us.
By teaching love,
we begin to affect their lives
and alter the course
and thought patterns of all we meet.

We will find that each circle of love
will overlap another
until all exist in a world of love.

Light Seeds

1. What obstacles prevent you from understanding the true na
ture of humanity?
2. List 5 ways you can be the source of your life.
3. Which "programs" have you brought into this life? How do
they affect your world?
4. List 5 events in your life that have helped your grow.
5. Where does the strength and the direction to grow come from
in your life?
6. List 5 benefits of leading a spiritual life.
7. List 4 choices you have made to achieve peace in your life.
8. List 4 obstructions to peace in your life.

14

Inner Path

"Every hardship;
every joy;
every temptation is a challenge of the Spirit;
that the human soul may prove itself.
The great chain of necessity wherewith we are bound has divine
significance;
and nothing happens which has not some service
in working out the sublime destiny of the human soul."

Elias A. Ford

What is this inner path? Why is it so important? How does it affect my life? I pondered these questions for years without finding an answer. I toiled; and became frustrated and worried because I could not sense its way in my life. But as time passed, I began to realize the inner landscape of my world. I achieved this realization after persistent and continual study. I learned how to center, focus and direct my life. After many years of listening for answers, I saw that this landscape forms a mural that spans eternity and is the world that creates love, finds peace, and provides a solace to the troubled soul.

Suffer not,
smile always.
Remember within is the pureness of life,
beauty,
and charm.

Watch your inner world,
listen to it
and be pleased with what you hear.

When you know your inner path
you will live your life in joy.
For when you watch over your self,
you will become freed
from the mindless worry of the fool.

You see,
You encompass all that can be.
You are the culmination of millennia of becoming.
You are the consummation of the Creator's love.
You are the strength of the ages.
You are able to uncover the dynamics of the universe.

As you travel your path,
you will notice that love,
caring,
and compassion
are the things that are necessary to achieve peace.
Therefore,
continue in your life's journey for these qualities
and know that you can succeed with the power
given to you by the universe.

Allow this power to flow through you
each moment of every day,
for when you allow the goodness of the universe
to flow through you,
you will be at peace.

If you could keep the Spirit's love foremost in your mind,
if you could dwell upon this love
as an example to follow,
if you could love as the Spirit loves,
your life would become a landmark for others to follow.

Learn to entrust your becoming to this love.

Begin to enlist your self in this quest for truth
and live each day with love.

Above all,
love each other with a passion
and travel with love as your guide.

Take a moment and consider the need for compassion
and the power of love in our lives. We need this power to
continue on our journey. We must work to put these feelings together in this life to make it whole, for it is being
whole that allows us to grow. All parts of life must connect
as a puzzle. Once we fit the pieces together, we will be able
to do astonishing things. You are each a piece to the master
puzzle and, as such, are part of the whole. That is why it is
important to learn of love. As you develop love and see its
rewards, you will notice that the total picture you create
will show all the love within each part. This can occur by
one individual changing his or her perspective, for one leads
to the love of another. By remembering the Spirit's love
and the effect you can have individually on the whole, you
will work to strengthen the whole by spreading love and
joy to everyone you meet.

Allow each puzzle piece to fall together with love
and build the picture of your soul with care.
Once completed,
the picture you see will transform your life.

When you see your soul in action,
you will become amazed at the love,
caring,
compassion,
and feelings that this love produces.

You will become at peace when you identify
and touch the hand of your soul.

We are to learn how to be prosperous as we move forward in life. Then, we are to walk gently each step of the way hand in hand with the Spirit. By doing this, we will accomplish all we do in life with love and compassion. We will become free and at peace. We will walk humbly with dignity throughout our lives and will learn to be without concern about our future. Then, we will receive the love that the universe sends our way by walking toward the Light. By accepting this Light, we will find that the universe provides all that we need each moment of our lives. Therefore, watch your path and notice where it leads. Notice the people you meet and the pleasures you experience, because these signal the boundaries of your path. Can you stop for a moment and think of your path's boundaries? I don't mean the physical boundaries of your outer world, but the inner boundaries of self. How do you enlarge its boundaries or create a safe place to be?

You entrust your self to the Spirit's Will
to become at rest.

You continue on the way you have chosen in life
and deliver your self new experiences each day.

You move aside the failures of yesterday
and begin the new challenges that each day brings.

You challenge your self to many different experiences.
Challenge your self to grow fully,
then,
work to uncover the needed lessons
that your life provides.

When we allow our selves to evolve, we allow the time necessary to learn and study all the lessons that life provides. You see, we do not arrive at our place in life by accident. We consciously lead our lives in the direction we choose in life. This ability to choose is one of the greatest secrets of life. What we think today will become the reality of our tomorrows for we consciously move in the direction of our thoughts. Therefore, think of positive and constructive ways to move through life as this will enhance your journey on this plane.

Take a moment and consider where you are today. Think of where you were before you began your journey. Don't you see a progression and a direct link between your thoughts before your journey began and your reality now? You will signal the direction of your quest by the inner thoughts you have and will use these thoughts working for the deliverance of your dreams into your life. You do this by consciously moving in the direction of your thoughts.

I looked carefully at the events that occurred throughout my life. Did I wish them to happen? What if I felt depressed by some event in my life? Would I attract depressing people to me? Of course I would! So, learn to be pleasant and kind, become cheerful and remove any ill feelings you may have toward another. By doing this, you will attract like individuals to your path. When you watch your path and the direction in which you travel, you will discover that your direction will be a clue to the inner voice you hear.

Listen to your inner voice that shows you the way.

Listen carefully to the direction given by your soul and follow the guidance you hear.

That small quiet voice is the most powerful leader you can imagine.

Quiet.
small.
still.
It is these things that produce power.

When you are strong in thought,
kind in action,
and walk within your soul,
you will lead a different life.
You will answer all of the questions
that life gives to you with joy
and will work to fulfill your part in this world.

Do not become discouraged when you
fail to perfect your desires,
for you will have time throughout eternity to develop.
Just take the time necessary to learn to develop your soul
and travel along your path in peace.

Use your life to enter into the world to love everyone
you meet. By showing this love, you will begin to change
the reality around you and will begin a revolution. Be thankful for the ability the Spirit has given you to change your
world. Allowing your self the ability to change and grow
allows you to increase your position in the universe.

By working out the karma in your life
your abilities will steadily grow.
Your self-confidence will be renewed.
You will become aware of changes that occur around you
and will see the Spirit within at work.

In this manner,
you will accomplish all.

For once you look within and listen,
you change your life forever.
Once you take that small step,
you will never be the same,
for the thought patterns of your mind
will be changed forever.

This change produced radical new ideas in my life. I knew the need in my life for others and began to part from those who caused difficulty or pain. I now surround my self with those who give me life and energy and take the time necessary to absorb the Spirit's love sent to me. I follow its inner teachings, for they are the thoughts that will allow me to grow the fastest and to move the farthest along my path. I see that good is found in all people and that all people need to be recognized and loved. I give everyone the space necessary to be who they are and give to them the love I give my self. I have learned to be happy for another's joy and to celebrate the joy found within both our lives. When I do these things, I travel within the Spirit and become at peace and know that the Spirit is with me always. When you travel within, you will think of others and will talk and act from peaceful and calm surroundings. You will find that this path alone will make the greatest difference in your life, for the Spirit's love is the greatest strength known in the universe. The uncovering of this fact provides you all the love possible in this universe and places joy within your being.

Light Seeds

1. How does your inner path affect your life? List 4 ways.
2. How do you interconnect with others to create a world of love?
3. List 5 things that the Light provides in your life.
4. Describe your journey to the present point. Then, detail the progression of this journey.
5. List 5 changes directly attributed to the Spirit in your life.

15

Spirituality

"Spirituality engenders creativity,
disciplining the mind,
heart and body.
With it you won't be preoccupied with the things you can't change,
and you can center your efforts on the things that make a difference...
asking how my time can be improved
and how things can be made more beautiful and useful."

Harold Glen Clark

Once you nurture your soul you will find an ability to transform your world. You will walk with your mind's eye on the Spirit's love and receive all the strength you need on your travel. Such love is wonderful, for when you call upon the Spirit you will obtain a lessening of the inner tension of your world and will perceive clearly that you are not alone. You will walk the road you are taking in peace. Become cheerful and do not allow your self to be embroiled in everyday circumstances, for in doing this you fail to choose your life's perspective based on eternity. Simply begin to center your mind on eternity and dwell within its bounds for eternity is the Spirit's gift to you.

It is our duty to work each day to overcome any evil we see in our world. It is by concentrating upon the good that is all around us that we will find the overall pattern of our lives starting to improve. There is immeasurable good in this world; good that is overlooked because of the narrow-mindedness of us all. When you work each day in the Spirit's shadow, you will experience an unlimited joy. This joy is the key to your life and to your survival on this realm. Think about your needs and desires and compare them to the needs and desires of eternity. Doing this will guide you into the proper frame of mind and direction in which to grow.

My way is stable and is a gift of the Spirit found within

me. When I think of this gift and allow it to enter my life, all the events that I encounter fall into proper order. I search my soul for messages left from ages past, for I find these messages valuable in my training. Then, I learn to become a synthesis of my past, present, and future, for I am moving into a dimension where peace and understanding abound. Spirituality causes a change in my life's attitude and this change will be the proper place to begin my journey. When I work on this attitude, I watch and see everything around me change. This allows me to see the good that comes to those who change their attitudes and learn to honor Spirit.

We each have a distance to go before our journey is complete, but each life begins with the quiet decision to move forward. Each day we take steps along that journey and move closer to our real and true selves. When we seek the spiritual in our lives, we discover the importance of our soul. This causes the ego, who is marshaling all its power against us, to fade away and allow us to become free. We gain this freedom when we constantly focus our minds and lives upon the Spirit. Therefore, begin to enter the Spirit and draw strength from associating with it, for it is only through diligent effort that you break the bounds held by your ego.

Begin each day by centering and focusing your mind.
Use that time to strengthen your soul's hold on your life
and begin to turn away the wishes of your ego self
and become at peace.

Each evening,
take time to empty your mind through meditation
and the honest development of peace.
By doing this,
you will give your soul your life and mind
and will begin to honor the self
as the reflection of the Spirit within.
This action will bring you peace in abundance.

Can you see that the pain you feel is the result of the difference between your reality and the reality you seek? Let go of this difference and realize that you will reach the vision you seek for your self, and that in doing this, you will free your self from any pain that you experience in life.

When you feel discouraged,
confer with the Spirit.

When you are not at peace,
confer with the Spirit.

You will struggle until you fully understand
that your soul is your true self
and allow it to direct your life.

Forget the ego
and remember the soul.
Then,
begin to work with your soul to uncover
the miracles given to you in this life.

In this very moment we can be at peace for we have a garden of unlimited beauty all around us. Learn to till the soil of your life and by living the spiritual life to watch this garden grow. Begin to tend it daily so that it will not grow the weeds of the past. Each day, place fertilizer on its fields and learn to hoe the areas that are in need of cultivation. Only through daily watching and gardening will your crops be abundant and healthy. Allow the Spirit to be with you each day as you center and focus your life. You will discover that this is the way and the path of Light.

You are here to learn certain lessons
and must pass several tests before you pass fully
to the next level.

You will find that each level will open in a way
and at a rate that can be absorbed within.

I found that the first step in my quest was to learn not to allow the events of my day to ruin my tranquillity. Each time I passed through a level within, I noticed my outside world become upset. This happened because I was breaking down the old walls that kept me bound in the past. I welcomed these signs because I discovered that confusion and dismay were the first signs of my inner growth.

My next step was to grow farther away from the world in which I lived and to begin to dwell within the Spirit. I began and ended my day with a moment of meditation. Doing this allowed me to realize the wonder and joy of that day. As I practiced this lesson, I kept my mind centered and thus prevented the development of depression and pain.

Look at life differently.
Look at life with the eyes of the Spirit within.

Doing this
allows you to live each moment fully.
You will not worry about tomorrow's outcome,
for the Spirit will watch your way.

Light Seeds

1. Define spirituality in your life.
2. List 5 areas in your life where joy can be found.
3. List 4 ways you can strengthen the Spirit's influence in your life.
4. What single action will provide peace in abundance in your life?
5. What are the steps to growth you have encountered in your life?

16

Life's task

"Don't be fooled by the calendar.
There are only as many days in the year as we make use of.
One man can get a week's value out of a full year,
while another can get a full year's value out of a week."

Charles Richards

How many people experience life without the consciousness of their path. They struggle without direction and find their purpose clouded from view. Over time, they realize their mistake but fail in attempts to find a path to follow and become saddened and lost. They lose the energy to change their world. They fail to realize that it takes active work to progress forward on their path, and that by following their inner voice, they would discover how to spontaneously obtain results in their lives.

Do not try to force any issue in life because force only clouds your ability to grow and provides the grounds for disaster. Do not try to force life. Just live it daily and enjoy each moment. Approach life as a child by remembering the ease in which a child accepts life, then, see how adults create chaos in their lives. Doing this allows us to see the flow of events in life without judging our selves or the events. It causes us to distance our selves from events and to realize that they are external to us.

Settle any conflict you may have about your responsibilities on this plane so that you can become free from the burdens of life. You see, life is to be lived freely and without pain. It is up to each of us to dismiss the pain, reject the materialism of this world, and simplify our lives. We will see our true self for what it is and will see how it is separate from the issues that surround us. Then we will live in abundant peace.

Have you noticed the beauty of the world around you?

Have you viewed the world you pass each day?

Look into your self
to remember and enjoy the journey
and to live within the Spirit.

Take the time to remember the Spirit within your being and see how you can change another's world. Enter into this world to show love and compassion and to see how the Spirit will help you find strength for your journey. You see, inner peace is a beautiful thing. It is our journey to work and to live in peace, because when in peace, we will find limitless knowledge. By realizing its presence, we will begin to feel enrichment, joy and calm in our lives. We will not worry, fear, envy or seek competition when we lead our lives from the space of peace, because love is found there in abundance.

It is your choice to go forth from this moment with a new direction. You can use this direction to love all you meet with a new Light and to become free of your old self-image. Then, you can look around and notice the tasks others do daily. Look carefully and notice that they are performing them without regard to their real desires or feelings. They go about their daily work without thinking whether they could enjoy their lives more.

Remember to be in touch with your true self
and live from that space.
Learn to uncover your self
and be pleased at what you see.

Your true self is the beauty within.
Therefore,
allow your beauty to become evident.
It is a wonderful gift to others.

Stabilize your life by allowing your true self to be known. In doing this, you will aid your transformation. You will listen to the voice of your true self and learn to follow its advice. Can you think of times when it felt right to help another, or when you accomplished a helpful task? Do you remember how wonderful you felt? Can you remember times when you were not in touch with your soul?

Do things that bring you internal joy and reward
and relate to each other with love.
Show your true self to others
and live in a world of peace.

Remember the goodness of your true self and focus on the direction your life is taking, so that you may begin to forget the old self and old habits you once knew. In doing this, you will provide the space and the room to grow farther and will quiet your mind to focus on the thoughts of your soul. You will become a changed consciousness and remain at peace as long as you dwell on the thoughts given to you by your Creator. It is up to each of you to remember the choice you made to follow the Creator's call. When you follow this call, you learn to make tomorrow your best and use your enlightened state to make this moment in your life new and exciting.

Light Seeds

1. What can you do to create a conscious path?
2. What can you do to eliminate conflict?
3. What can others teach you about direction?
4. What is the stabilizing factor in your life?

17

Your Role

"To look is one thing,
to see what you look at is another,
to understand is still something else,
but to act on what you hear
is all that really matters!

Author Unknown

After I spent time discovering my inner world, it was necessary to use the wisdom I gained to affect my outer world. This wisdom comprises our path and makes it unique for each of us. The path of wisdom is the path to follow in life, for it leads to the Light and into the Spirit's love. This journey will bring satisfaction and will lead to a lifetime of joy and happiness. I gain much throughout my journey by working with other souls and helping them alter their passage in life. By working together we will participate in the changing of the universe from one of confrontation to one of love. By helping others we help ourselves, which begins the awakening of both our souls and directs our paths into the Light.

Each of us plays a part in this saga.
Each of us has a message to bring to the world.
Each of us responds to the call
to expand our consciousness.

Listen for the call
and remain at peace for eternity.

Aligning our minds to the eternal focuses our lives on the worthy intent of our souls. Focusing upon the good in this universe allows us to succeed in identifying the best our souls have to offer. It is during the days we feel the greatest sorrow that our minds will focus on the things we need to change in our lives. Perhaps there is a goal you need to focus on such as a deep-seated fear or emotional need. Do not look at these events with dismay, but realize that each event is an opportunity to see where you need to grow and focus. Become aware of these moments and learn to grow from them for by working each day on the growth of your soul, you will focus on your vision.

Do not allow pain to slow down your progress or cause you to waver from your decision to grow. Pain comes from the pressure you place upon your self to change into a different person and is due to your desire to change your life into one based on your soul's message. Allow your self the time to adjust and the time to acclimate your self to the new thought patterns of your soul.

Enjoy your journey.
Enjoy the burdens of everyday life.
These are what teach.
These are the things that cause you to continue to grow.
Without them,
you would not have the courage to move forward
because courage remains dormant until it is mobilized.

Place these words in your heart:

Go in the direction of your soul
and you will have peace.
Walk slowly
and with direction.
Then,
study your path each day
and do not deviate from your chosen course.

It is important to become at peace with the direction of your life and not make the mistake of comparing your self to others. Remember, the Spirit directs your soul's destiny and you must follow your destiny to its completion. Do this by working one day at a time to bring your life's purpose to fruition.

Light Seeds

1. List 5 ways you can affect your world? Do these comprise your role in life?
2. List 5 ways you can align your mind to the eternal.
3. What difference will this have on your life?
4. When you compare yourself to others, how do you feel? Is it worth the pain?

18

Materialism

"Thinking to get at once all the gold the goose could give, he killed it and opened it only to find—nothing."

Aesop

The physical plane is full of insecurity and can lead us away from the Spirit. Our ability to touch, feel and experience creates the desire to have tangible things in our lives. The act of being physical produces the need for material goods and creates a diversion from the real world of love. We need to become focused and centered on our true selves in order to remove materialism as the focal point of our lives. By looking from this perspective, we see how the material life can cause us to follow a path that could cause great harm and misery.

Therefore,
always go in the direction of your soul.
Always progress onward
and do not become distressed
by any perceived lack of progress.

Some progress is from within
and cannot be seen outwardly.
Such progress is the most fulfilling kind
and is what you need to develop spiritually.

Become enlightened by listening carefully to inward signs. Listen and watch for signs of inner growth to experience continued fulfillment in life. See the need to let go of the materialism that is so prevalent on this plane. Letting go of materialism allows us to discover that all we need is our inner love, for such love is all we could ever want in life. You see, we do not need to own everything. In fact, we cannot own everything and still have possession of our souls. Many sell their souls to have the possessions they wish. Do your possessions create joy or do they bring dissatisfaction with life? Become aware of the joy around you and notice how joy is not attached to your possessions.

We all differ in our beliefs. Some are not content to live by spiritual standards because spiritual standards are not tangible things. We cannot see, read, or show spirituality to anyone except in the way we live and operate our lives. This manner of living is not as exciting as the life that materialism may provide. But do not be surprised, because spirituality will outlast any gratification that materialism can give. Remember, our legacy is for eternity and we are building a life based on the foundation of the Spirit. This legacy will withstand all difficulties and hardships that life can present to us.

Take a moment to look at others' lives and see how unhappy they are. Do they know who they are? Do they feel harmony within because they have found true spiritual peace? Do they understand the principles of the universe? The answers to these questions are obvious to those who take the time to see their world.

Our responsibility in life is to become at peace with our standing in this universe. Do not settle for second place in life because you will find that there isn't a second place in the spiritual world. Our place on this plane is to provide teaching and to become more of what we truly are. We are to become more of our selves each moment of our lives and to continue to develop it forever. It is amazing that we cannot become too much. We can only become. This is a rule that outweighs anything found in the materialistic world. In the material world, you can only grow to certain heights; however, in the spiritual world there is no limit to the ability to grow. The spiritual journey is a miracle and is worth spending our lives to pursue.

Thus,
walk without fear in your life.
You are on the path that only your Creator can understand
and are doing things in your life others cannot envision.
Be pleased with this growth potential.

Dwell on the spiritual in your life for you will find that all other things will fall by the wayside. Be your self and disregard the pressures placed upon you each day to accommodate your life to the material world. When you let go of all the teachings of the material world, joy will reign supreme in your life. You are created perfect. Therefore, realize how you can develop more and more joy and happiness when you concentrate on your spiritual path.

It takes courage to become free of the bondage of this world because we are constantly being prodded to conform. This pressure can be a problem for those on the spiritual path because the spiritual path is not an easy path, nor is it a path that all can follow. It is, however, the only path that leads to everlasting happiness and peace. Too many try to overcome the pain of this world by withdrawing or hiding from issues, yet the opposite is necessary. We can become part of this world, remain separate from it, and overcome the materialism of this day. This action is essential to clearing our minds and souls of the clouded information we receive from our world.

We are on a course toward higher consciousness and should begin to live our lives according to the spiritual principles we uncover. Take time to be thankful each day for the lives we lead and to be thankful for the many lessons that we are able to learn. This tool is essential to obtaining eternal peace, for we must give up this world to gain our lives. Become watchful and become at peace with the life you lead and learn to accept the small miracles you see each day. Once you do, you will begin each day with the Spirit's love within your heart and will see the peace of its goodness in your soul.

You are the essence of your Creator.
You are the only commentary necessary
on the way life should be.

Work to make the world a better place
and to see the difference you can make.

Work each day to understand the reasons
for problems you encounter
and become more positive in your relations with others.

Be confident in the direction you are taking in life.

In doing this,
you will work each day to uncover
and bless the direction your soul takes.

Look with great satisfaction upon the life you lead
and the life that is to be.
For you are constantly changing
and providing to others new glimpses
of life and life's relationships.

Become all that you can be.
Settle for nothing.
But,
work for all.

Work each day to understand more and more of the needs that surround you. By doing this, you will remain at peace with any decisions you make in life. You will know that you are succeeding along your path and will not allow your self room to worry or regret any part of your journey. All new lessons appear to be impossible when we first attempt them. However, when we work on our visions with diligence, we can achieve them and complete all the lessons given to us. Become happy and in charge of your life, because tomorrow some may try to disturb you or alter your path. When they do, tell them about the decisions you have made to correct your path.

We become as great as we allow our selves to be because we each hold a picture of our selves within our minds. This picture develops over many years and is present to help us remain focused on our life's course. Make sure that the picture you have in front of your eyes is the correct one, for the correct picture is needed to maintain the proper focus on your life. You see, whatever this picture shows determines the outcome of your life. So, make sure this picture shows you the outcome you wish to obtain.

Work on this picture,
refine its focus.
As you consistently see this picture before your eyes,
the world about you will conform to its image.

Light Seeds

1. List 5 ways materialism prevents you from living a spiritual life.
2. How does society prod you to conform? List 4 ways.
3. What picture do you hold of your self in your mind?
4. How does that picture affect your world?
5. How can you change it?

19

Thankfulness

"Never lose an opportunity of seeing anything that is beautiful;
for beauty is God's handwriting—a wayside sacrament.
Welcome it in every fair face,
in every fair sky,
in every fair flower,
and thank God for it as a cup of blessing."

Ralph Waldo Emerson

Act like a magnet and draw people to you
who have the same interests as you.

Draw them close
and discuss thoughts that will empower them.

Walk among them
and know that your path is leading you to the Light.

Look for the Light
and follow it closely.

Speak of the Light
and tell others of the goodness found within it.
Then,
center your mind on the Spirit
and realize the peace it provides.

I find it important to follow the Light every moment of
each day and to make each day as perfect as possible. By
focusing and making each day perfect, I believe that each
tomorrow and each successive month, year, century and age
will become perfect in turn. Therefore, focus on the present
moment and make it perfect, for by doing this you will create a perfect future.

We are here to make the best of this life and to learn all the lessons presented to us. In so doing, we become more spiritual and in tune with the universe. We become more open, happy, peaceful, and are sought by others because of the calm they see around us. Our aura shines. Our being glitters. All around us people see our radiance and as they see this difference in our lives, they draw closer to us.

This is the way to live
and the way to grow.

Find your way
and look for your path.

Inner peace opens my life to eternity and allows me to see the Light of my Creator. Seeing this Light removes the fear, anger, frustrations and ego so that I can replace them with love and compassion. By doing this, I help all whom I can on their path and help them learn to become a soul of Light. This is the message from Spirit: *Become a soul of Light.* Don't spend your life telling others of this Light when you can live the Light each day. Live, breathe and become the Light so that you may become the maker of your destiny and the creator of your path. Know that you are the fabricator of your world and will ultimately be the creator of your fate.

Our walk is to study the Spirit's path and to realize that we are showing others the way to be and to live. Others have the responsibility to do likewise. In accepting this responsibility, our love will be seen by all we contact and will inspire others on their path to create moments of peace. Use these moments as an inspiration to each other and allow them to know the wonder you see in the universe and in your life.

Add together all the times you could have seen wonders
but did not.

Add together all the times you could have helped others
but did not.

Add together all the times you could have grown
but did not.

Make a pact to
begin from this day to grow
and mature spiritually.
Grow this moment by realizing your position
and placement in the universe.
Then,
look with new eyes at the wonder that surrounds you.

The results of doing this will astound you and will focus your life on the Spirit within, as you allow the Spirit to
enter your conscious world.

This is what makes life worthwhile.

This is what makes your lifetime important.

Each small event that is present causes you to grow.
Each small moment of time adds up to eternity.

Use your life to absorb the abundance of the universe
present within your soul.

See it,
feel it
and live it each moment of every day.
By doing this,
you will use each event to show you the way.

You will see each event as a miracle in disguise.
You will begin to see the Spirit within each moment
and within each life you touch.

At the end of each day I give thanks for the goodness that the universe has brought my way. I am aware of this goodness and let all around me know my gratitude by changing the fabric and makeup of my world. I pay attention to this small detail and witness my life change forever.

Make this passing on the Earth your best.

Make it full of surprise and wonder.

Grow each moment of your life
to see the beauty that surrounds you.

These are the things
that will make your world worthwhile.
These are the moments
that will produce peace and contentment in your life.

Begin to see your world as you wish to see it. Focus on every aspect of that vision and remember it quietly each day. Thus, you will see it slowly mature before you.

This is the way to change your world.

Do not make broad speeches or proclamations to others,
but quietly,
little by little,
piece by piece,
focus daily.
Focus throughout eternity.
Focus always upon the Light.

Light Seeds

1. List 5 ways you can show thankfulness in your life.
2. List 4 ways you can show gratitude to others.
3. If you fully lead a spiritual life, how will your life change?

4. What steps can you take to change your world to live in the Spirit?

20

Soul

"If that vital spark that we find in a grain of wheat
can pass unchanged through countless deaths and resurrections,
will the spirit of man be unable to pass from this body to another?"
                                        William Jennings Bryan

Embark on your journey called life
with enthusiasm and love.
Embark with thoughts of helping others.
By helping them,
you will cause a change in the direction of their lives
and will move toward the Light.

Work each day to surround your self with people
who will cause you peace
and contentment.
Then,
continue in the direction of the Light
and in the direction of your soul.

The Spirit is the Light and in it we will grow and prosper. With its help, we will grow and cause a change in the direction of our world. When we use the energy given to us to do good for others and to improve the world in which we live, we will encounter all foes with the love that the Spirit provides. Use this knowledge from the Spirit to impart to others the existence of a new society that will encompass spiritual values in the structure of its heart. Then, consider in quiet the movement of our souls and their needs and desires.

Consider your soul. It has been present since the beginning and has nourished you throughout eternity. It is present to show the Spirit's love to everyone around you and through the soul your world is altered. When you take time to wel-

come the soul into the reality of your daily experience, it
will have its greatest effect upon your life.

Consider your souls' desire
and consider its message in your daily walk.
Watch your life grow as you contact your soul.
Use the knowledge it provides to improve your ways
and the direction of your life.

Allow your soul the freedom
and the ability to lead you
into the world that surrounds you.

By listening to your soul,
you will become a more healing person
and you will become your true self.

Your soul is beautiful. It has many parts that make up
the whole. Part of the soul is in constant communication
with the Creator, while another part is independent and free
to make choices. Yet another is in communication with your
being and still another is in tune with the universe about
you. Attract all these parts and make them the whole of
your being. When you do, you will open your heart to the
messages of your soul and will know that you are the Spirit's
child placed on earth to create beauty and love.

Interpret your soul's intent within your life.
Absorb its beauty and wisdom within your being.
Uncover the wishes of the soul
and live daily by the principles it provides.
Uncover within your soul the beauty placed by the Spirit
and know that it is good.
Then,
begin to worship the Spirit
and welcome it within.

For it is through the soul's voice
that the Spirit will manifest itself
and become a part of your being.

I look at the changes in my life that my soul causes. In doing this, I see directly the miracle of the Spirit's love. I use this love and know that my Creator is the maker and the designer of all I encounter. I welcome the Spirit into my life and know that all my being is a part of its beauty. It only takes listening to my soul for the picture of the Spirit's direction to appear.

Listen quietly for the message and love of the Spirit.
This will direct your path to the One who has created
all that surrounds you.
This is the promise given at your conception
and is the notice given each day of your life.

Work to make the Spirit within visible.
Work to make its love a portion of your life.
Then,
work to know that it is the one and only arbitrator
you need in your life.
This will allow you to
worship the Spirit in all it's beauty
and see the world change about you.

All the universe seeks its love,
knows its presence,
and knows its wisdom.
Therefore,
know that all is good
when the Spirit is in your midst.

The Spirit will cause us to live lives that are happy and prosperous. We will become new and discover how the Spirit causes us to make a difference in our lives. We will encourage the empowerment of our hearts and will envision the new world we wish to create. This will attest to all around us the unfolding of our soul into the world and will allow us to see the true function of our lives.

Light Seeds

1. What is your definition of soul?
2. List 5 ways your soul affects your life.
3. What does your soul feel like?
4. What is its intent in your life?
5. List 5 changes that you can attribute to your soul.

21

Transitions

"Why build these cities glorious
If man unbuilded goes?
In vain we build the world
Unless the builder also grows."

Edwin Markham

All of life is a series of transitions. We are born, develop, mature, die and pass on to others the wisdom we obtain during each lifetime. In doing this, we cause a change in the relations we have with others and enlarge our perspective of the universe. Take the time to study the events of your past, then allow them to fade from view. By learning the lessons of your past and working to make today your best, you will change the matrix of your present moment of time, and thus, cause a change in the direction of your world.

Become steady, become trustworthy, and become knowledgeable in the ways of the universe. Study the ways of your Creator and apply them to the universe at large. By doing this, you will walk gently through this world. You will use the knowledge you uncover to expand your role and your enlightenment, and thus, expand your abilities on this plane.

Realize that you are limitless.
Realize that you can have all that you wish.
Realize that your future is as unlimited as space itself.
Then,
go and create that change.

The Spirit provides change as the element that allows growth, for we are capable of instantaneous change. We are given free will and as such are allowed to create our world.

When we do not like the way we find a situation, we can always change our direction and attitude and thus change its outcome.

Change your world so that all things for good
are accomplished.
Then,
change your mind about the material things of this world.

Realize that growth is the reason for your being
and that growth in any other direction but the spiritual
is fruitless and without foundation.

Look at your world and study the people you see. Look and see changes that are needed, then go and change them. You may need to change friends, lifestyles, occupations or circles of influence. Anything that stands in the way of your developing toward the spiritual will cause you to dwindle instead of grow.

Remember your reason for being
and spread love among all your fellow humans
to encourage others to become.

Your soul has the answers
if you only listen.

Your soul has the way
and the means to satisfy your life
for living within the eternal
changes the perspective of your life.

Listen intently to all you hear.
Catalog within your mind all the Spirit's news.
This is the way to use its knowledge.

Allow this knowledge to filter within your soul.

Once awakened, people will rally around you and raise your level of consciousness. Allow them to know your abilities because you will use their questions to help you learn of your self and, through them, accept your responsibility to grow and prosper.

Look within
to find the secret of all times.

Look within
and know that the Creator is present in your life.

Look around
and see the people who deny
the Spirit's presence in their lives.
Then,
become comforted that you are on the path
and can watch the future closely
for in your future lies all the things you desire.

Today,
you must begin.
You must learn to continue on with the Spirit.
Remember the special qualities of each person you meet
and how their qualities differ.
Use your abilities to their fullest
and impart love and caring to everyone each day.

We can affirm to those we meet that the happiness found in life is due to the peace that is found in the Spirit. In its shadow and in the wisdom of the universe, goodness reigns, peace abounds, and love prevails. When we listen carefully to all the words that we receive from our souls, we will see the difference they can make in our world.

Walk within your soul
and see beauty.

Walk within another's soul
and help raise their level of consciousness.

Tell others of your love.
Tell others how you appreciate them.
Tell them to become all they can be.
Then,
each day improve your life by a small amount.

Each day learn to grow a little.
Over days,
weeks and months.
you will change your world.

I am thrilled at the ability I have to change my world. I
notice the richness that is present when I walk within my
soul. I learn to help others overcome the human qualities
they possess and supplement these qualities with the news
of the Creator's love.

Work to improve your environment,
to improve your relations with others,
to improve your self daily,
and to improve the atmosphere of your world.

Grow to help others.
Grow to become.
Grow to be
and become at peace.

You will go into the world a new person
because you have willed it so.

You will go into the universe
and allow others to know that you are whole.

Continue to listen to the words given by your soul and study any thoughts it presents to you. Doing this is the biggest step. The next step is the assimilation and the use of this news.

You will
become all you can
and grow each day.

You will live each day to uncover your true self within
and will work to improve the circumstances
in which you live.

When you make this lifetime the best possible
you have succeeded greatly.

It is time to go into the world,
make a difference,
and change its thoughts.

Go into the world
and change the patterns present over the ages

This change is good
and is valuable.
This change is necessary to save this planet.
This change is coming
and it is wonderful,
for the Spirit's love is its cause.

Light Seeds

1. What has helped you the most as you have traveled through the transitions of your life?
2. How can you help others during their transitions?
3. List 5 changes you will make in your world during this transition.

22

Souls of Light

"Day and Night;
and every moment;
there are voices about us.
All the hours speak as they pass;
and in every event there is a message to us;
and all our circumstances talk with us;
but it is in divine language;
that worldliness misunderstands;
that selfishness is frightened at;
and that only the children of God hear rightly and happily."
William Mountford

It is up to each of us to teach ourselves of the world around us. We need to look for minor changes that we can make each day, for in making small changes results will occur over time. Each day, if we cause a small change to occur in our attitude or in our direction, we will notice in the end that profound changes have occurred.

Look for miracles in your world because each day they occur but go unnoticed. You work and live on life's stage and perform for other people. Make your performance one that will cause them to wonder about the change that has occurred within you. Work each day to develop joy and peace within your mind and notice the lessons in life that you are learning. You must learn of the contributions your life makes to your world to realize the impact you have on the whole. Many times you feel that you do not contribute to the overall good of your world. You will discover that such thinking is flawed, for you have had many opportunities to contribute to your society. By thinking of the contributions you make, you will realize the areas of life you enjoy and understand. You will contribute much to each other and will cause your life to affect many people. You are a child of your Creator and as such do many great things. Realizing this allows you to focus on the good that you do for others and see how moments of love make up these events.

Cherish the friends you make in life.
Work to make their lives better
and more pleasant,
for you affect each of their lives
as quickly as you affect your own.

You are a part of the universal whole
and as such are capable of great things.
You can alter the fabric of creation
by thinking spiritual thoughts
and doing spiritual deeds.

Work each day to uncover the goldmine within your being. Work to uncover it and to show it to others. If you open your mind to the beauty and the gold around you, your life will take on a different focus. This is the reason Spirit is within you; for it is there to make a difference. It is there to accomplish great things.

Know that the direction you are taking in life is sweet. Isn't it wonderful that you can see and do so much? Concentrate on making each day the best you can. Then, think of ways you can help others to correct their misconceptions of their world. This is the way to alter the course of your world and to become whole.

Bring your way into the world and know that you are following the highest good spoken by your inner voice. In your subconscious lies all the wonders of your past and all the goodness of your future. Therefore, identify with this consciousness and learn to ask of it the news of each day. You will become one with this news and know that its message is for your best good.

Remove all the materialism of the world from your pain.

Remove all suffering.

What is left is the purest form of peace possible.

Therefore,
choose to remove the pain from your life.
It is gone very easily.
Then,
remember the truth about your soul self
and follow its voice.
When you do,
you will begin to look at things with kindness.
You will look and see a Spirit that others fail to see
and will welcome the peace you receive in return.

I continue to realize that each new morsel of knowledge I possess results in a profound change in my life. I recognize the peace I possess and work to increase it by showing love and caring to others. The true extent of my growth is measured by my ability to live on this road of peace and contentment.

Open your heart each day
to allow the entrance of the Spirit.

Open your mind to the reality that it provides,
for you can undo any hardship by listening to your heart.

You will understand the need for walks alone
and the need for moments of quiet and silence.

Listen to these moments
as they surround you in meditation.
Listen to the peace they provide in order to become.

You are present on this plane at this time in your life to learn many lessons. You are walking the spiritual road and are having difficulty realizing the new reality that surrounds you. When you feel lost, listen to your heart and work to allow it to speak. By doing this, you will become a real conduit of love in this world. You will perceive that your future is along the spiritual road and your way is on the path of Light.

Learn to enjoy each day,
to love one another,
and to be less serious about life.

Learn to laugh and sing.
You are alive
and this itself a wonder.
Continue to learn
and to know peace and contentment.
Understand the need for moments of concern
and the need to grow.
Do this by learning all the necessary lessons in life
so you will find what you seek in life.

Know these truths:

Work to perfect your life at this moment.

Do not allow tomorrow to cause you worry,
for tomorrow may never come.

Learn to settle arguments you have with love.
Then,
forgive all about you of any wrongdoing that may occur.
By doing this,
you will honor your Creator
and know that you are safe.

Begin to see that in allowing Light to enter our lives we allow our world to change. We create a fresh view of our surroundings and begin to live our lives differently. Look around and visualize scenes in your mind. See success and see love, caring and helping others as the real vision to pursue. How can such a way of life fail? How can such a beautiful way be tarnished? Work on the vision you see in this Light, for it is good. Know that within this Light is found the direction of the Spirit.

Learn to peel away the layers of yesterday and uncover the beauty of today. By doing this, you become aware of your place in the universe. Remove any blockage from your path and open the way to the future. Then, work for inner peace and know that it lives within your soul. Live for this peace to become content with life, for you will see that your life is precious, your love is endless, and your spirit is pure.

I enter into the future with the knowledge of the Creator's love within my heart. I enter this world as a new person and become free of the stress I once knew. I work moment to moment to eliminate stress and know that I am a child of the Spirit. I know that by loving one another we will learn to enter each day with thankfulness and will work to purify our soul's intent to become totally at peace.

It is time for you to walk in your life in peace and to know of your Creator's love. Spend each day in harmony with its path and *become a soul of light*. You do this by enlisting all the thoughts you possess in the creation of the reality you desire. So, work today and every day to produce and form this new reality. Take and work with all these abilities given you by your Creator and know that you are at peace in this world. When you begin to satisfy your wants with love and work to fulfill your life with peace, you will enter each day with the Creator's peace upon your lips.

Look upon the world you see
and listen to the beauty it provides.
Look upon the world as a complete being.

Work each moment to realize the truth of your self
and to realize the beauty that is within.
Enter each moment of life
with the determination to succeed
in your path through life.

Work to be.

Become a soul of Light. Work to uncover this path in all its beauty. By doing this, you will enter each day with joy and will win at all the encounters you face along your journey. You will find unknown ways to walk on your journey and will learn to be happy that the way is not fixed. You will find joy in the turns you discover on your road, for they are lessons and opportunities to grow and mature. This life process will allow you to see the progress you make and will allow others to be aware and in touch with your true self.

All that you can be is the correct path.
All that is possible is the Way.
Therefore,
go on your path without fear.
Go without danger,
for you are on the path given to you,
and it is good.

While traveling on this path, you will see your future before your eyes and know that it is in the Spirit's direction. You will work diligently in the direction of your dreams and will move in the direction of the development of your soul.

Listen always to your soul
for by doing this,
you will become at peace.

You have unimaginable beauty about you and your life's path stands for all the honorable things on this plane. You are succeeding by understanding the knowledge presented to you and now need to spend time listening to your inner soul, for by listening and learning, you will become.

Take the time to learn your lessons and to become your path. Slow down your direction and drive so you can hear your inner voice speak. Each of you must uncover the absolute peace found within your soul in order to walk gently in the way of your soul and become fully human. You see, the spiritual road is the eternal road and is found by those who seek. So, embrace your life with the goodness of your soul and find rest. By choosing the direction of your soul, you will travel in its way and find happiness.

This is your opportunity to go into the world and become.
Go into the world and teach.
Go into the world
and settle all the difficulties that surround you.
You are the true image of your Creator
and must allow the flow of the universe
to enter your daily thoughts.

You are searching for the truth. Others will search in incorrect places. Others will look at their reality and think that external things cause them great joy and happiness. It is the few who decide to look within and see the beauty given and made by the Creator who are truly happy. These are the people who make miracles happen.

Therefore,
take the time to search
and to find the joy of becoming.
Become all that you can be
and know that the path you follow is good,
honest,
and will lead you home.
Know that it will lead you
to *become a soul of Light.*

Light Seeds

1. List 4 miracles you have seen in your life.
2. How have they affected your life?
3. List 5 ways you can allow the Spirit to enter your life.
4. List 4 lessons you have learned so far in your life.
5. How can you become a soul of Light?

Epilogue

*"Produce great pumpkins,
the pies will follow later."*

Author Unknown

Integrating the events of your day with the soul's message allows you to learn to use your soul self to discover the true path you are to follow. Listening to your soul when you have doubts about your direction, allows you to become at peace with its response. When you listen to your soul during times of difficulty, you hear its whisper and focus on its message and begin to understand its call. At times you will notice its advice even before it is requested. This happens when you become in tune with your soul and are able to listen to your soul self as your guide. Do not expect quick answers to your concerns because sometimes such concerns can only be answered by learning through life's journey.

Each lifetime is different.
Each is unique.
Wonder at the diversity that each lifetime gives
and know that the lessons contained in each are for your
highest good.

Each of you can forge the future of a child
or mend a broken heart.
Therefore,
dwell upon the possibilities of your creation
and know that they are for the good of all.

Work each day to perfect the soul that you are.
Work each day to understand the miracle called life.
Spend each moment in quiet gratitude
for the challenges you are given.

Then,
undertake these challenges with joy.

Work with joy.
Live with joy.
For when you live your life
within the peace of the moment
you will know that all you do is good
and is for the betterment of your soul.

You will find that each moment is a lesson to be learned,
each day is a chapter in the book of life,
each moment is to be cherished
and to be blessed.

Work to make each day on this plane joyful
and full of plenty.
Work each day to uncover your soul in all its facets
and to help others in their walk.

We have mastered many things and have spent
untold moments learning the world's ways. Let's now
spend the remainder of our lives in celebration and as a
testament to the Creator's love. By doing this, we will see
how our souls can empower us to heights unknown, for
our souls can work wonders in our lives.

Light Seeds

1. List 5 ways you can integrate your soul's messages into
   your life.
2. List 5 ways you can use these messages to help others.

From the author of **Souls of Light**

A transformational audio cassette narrated by Dr. Ronald D. Bissell with original music by A.T. McHugh

Audiotape
$12.95
1 tape
1 hr. & 40 min.

Inner
Voice
PRODUCTIONS

To order, call or write INNER VOICE PRODUCTIONS at 1-800-428-1563 (1-800-427-1122 in Maine), Suite 2165, 2 Saco Island, Saco, Maine 04072, or use the order form on the following page.

From **Inner Voice Productions**

Wisdom and music from the soul

THE SOUL SPACE

$12.95
Audiotape

$10.95
Paperback

SOULS *Of* LIGHT

A Personal Guide to Spiritual Transformation

by Dr. Ronald D. Bissell

**To order THE SOUL SPACE or SOULS OF LIGHT,
call 1-800-428-1563 (1-800-427-1122 in Maine) or use this form.
(Please have your credit card handy when calling.)**

ORDER FORM FOR **The Soul Space** and **Souls of Light**

Name _____

Address _____

City _____ State _____ Zip _____

Phone (day) _____ (eve.) _____

Please send me #____ copies of **THE SOUL SPACE** at $12.95 each
and # ____ copies of **SOULS Of LIGHT** at $10.95 each. (All pay-
ments must be in U.S. dollars. Maine residents add 6% sales tax.
Add $3.00 shipping and handling to order total.) All orders
shipped first class mail within 48 hours of receipt.

☐ Payment enclosed $ _____

Charge my ☐ Visa ☐ Mastercard ☐ Discover

Card # _____ -- _____ -- _____ -- _____

Exp. Date _____ Signature _____

Please complete this form and mail in an envelope to:
Inner Voice Productions, Suite 2165, 2 Saco Island, Saco, Maine, 04072.